# SOUTHWICK-on-V

# Volume 4

by

## Peter Gibson

*To Mrs Florence Simpson 1923-1996*

"I never realised that there was history close at hand beside my very own home. I did not realise that the old grave that stood among the brambles at the foot of our farm was history"

*Steven Leacock*

British Library Cataloguing-in-Publication Data
A Catalogue record for this book is available from the British Library
ISBN 0-9513908-3-X

*Front Cover*

*Top left:* HRH Diana Princess of Wales gives a warm handshake to a young girl in the crowd on her visit to Southwick in 1990 (see back cover and page 102).

*Top right:* An early tinted photograph of the north side of The Green in about 1905.

*Top centre:* The earliest known view of The Green is this 1881 painting looking northwards by Southwick artist Robert Shanks. The village green has been recently laid out using funds raised by public subscription. Trees were planted and grass seed sown. Wooden railings enclose The Green but soon they were torn own, the saplings uprooted and the new grass destroyed. Photographs taken at the turn of the 20th century show the barren state of the village green (see Vol 1).

Launch sequence of the *Johanna Oldendorff* at the Southwick Shipyard early in 1986 (Pictures by welder Dave Aldridge).

*Bottom left*: James Edward Foster, Air Gunner, aged twenty-three, of Hawthorne Street, Carley Place, was killed in a collision of aircraft in December 1944.

*Middle right:* Mayor of Sunderland, Southwick Councillor Bryan Charlton is pictured after he opened the restored Southwick Council Offices building in March 1994. He is holding bound volumes of the Southwick-on-Wear book which was presented to him as a memento of the occasion (see page 99).

# Acknowledgements

Alan Brett (Black Cat Publications) and Andrew Clark for their professional help and advice. My grateful thanks for their co-operation and hard work at the production stage of this book.

Historian Tom Corfe for his guidance and comments on the text; and from whom I have learnt as much.

Alan Tedder (East End historian) for indexing 1930s newspaper articles about Southwick for me.

Artist Pal Palmer for his line drawings.

Terry Gibson for help with the Gibson family history, and help when photographing Southwick scenes.

Phil Hall Sunderland City Library (Local Studies).

Hills Bookshop of Waterloo Place.

Mrs Irene Gibson for proofreading, and for putting up with it all.

Mark Gibson for his comments on the text in the chapter 'Suddick Roots and Childhood Memories.'

My grateful thanks to the subscribers to this book who are listed on pages 103 & 104.

The *Sunderland Echo* for allowing me to reproduce several of their photographs and articles.

For photographs, information and other help:

Sunderland Museum & Art Gallery, Neil Sinclair, Judy Sunley, Alison Ross, Martin Routledge, the Museum Attendants for their help and co-operation, Pat O'Brien, Harry & Ann Bruce, Alf & Joan Davison, Aerofilms Ltd, Tony Smith, Alan Brett, Peter, Tom & Jim Clark, Jim Weatherill, Les Cooper, Jack Washington, Gordon Howe, Jossy Wilson, Mrs Elizabeth Stead, Mary Shaw, Bob Graham, Margaret Lancaster, family of Mrs Price of the Banks of the Wear pub, Lewis Carroll's family, Mr & Mrs Ellison, Norman Wilkinson, Tom Cunningham, Leslie & Joan Tate, Derek Thompson, Mrs Esther Gibson, Benjamin S. Brazier, Ministry of Defence, Jimmy Langley, Nance Gibson, Pearce Gibson, Sir Charles Madden, E.A. Rogers, Billy Evans, Dr David Evans, George Gibson, John Wolfe, Ron Giles, Billy Pemberton, Tommy Thompson's Album, Alan Burnett, Steve Speak, Arthur Turnbull, Ian S. Carr, Sunderland AFC, Tommy Keegan, Christina Ward, Tucker Mooney, A & P News, Iris Lindsay, the late Billy Donkin, Michael Henry, historian Stuart Miller, Mrs Lilian Fletcher, Mr & Mrs Sallabanks, Mrs Wilkinson, Tom Bland, Mr & Mrs Bambrough, Miss Margaret Lennon, Mrs Hetherington, Norman Hunter, Cath Fenwick, Mrs Anne Ray, Brian Scott, Greta Pyburn, Mrs Marie Foster, Derek Smith, David Warne, George Atkinson, Mr Ken Lay, Mrs Farrer, Alfred Ibbitson, Peter Aslett, Mrs Mary Farnsworth, Billy Tate, Mrs Elsie Cairns, Wilfred Taylor, Alan Marshall, Mrs Marshall, Robert M. Laybourn, Doreen Wilkinson, Mrs Catherine Harper, Jean & Brian Stephenson, Michael Gibson, Mrs Annette Swinburne, Mrs Gertrude Garraway, Sally Collins, Mrs Nora Pearn, Harry Rowley, Elsie Forbister, Ann Gregg, Shauna Gregg, Mary Evans, Linda O'Brien, Mr M. Gatenby, Olive Herkes, Carol Grieves, Billy Pearn, Mr & Mrs Hawkey, Mrs Smith (nee Price), Mrs Irene Cook, Dorothy Barkes, Doreen Talbot, Mr & Mrs Fred Veitch, Rev Robert Dixon, Birmingham City Library, Ashley Sutherland, Staff of C35 General Hospital.

**Newspapers and Sources**

Sunderland Daily Echo

Sunderland Times

Sunderland Herald

Sunderland Weekly News

The Corder Manuscripts

Southwick Council Minutes

Trade Directories

Census Returns (1841 to 1891)

Sunderland Museum & Art Gallery

Sunderland City Library (Local Studies)

Hendon Branch Library

Various maps of Southwick available in Sunderland Museum and City Library Local Studies

Oxford Dictionary of National Biography (1931-1940)

Golfiana Volume 5 Number 2 (1993)

# Contents

Acknowledgements 2

Foreword by Tom Corfe 4

Farming Lives 5

The 1870s

I. Some Developments and the Local Boards 11

II. Drunkenness, Violence and Some Strange Goings On! 20

Characters and Personalities 25

Lewis Carroll, A Walrus, A Carpenter and Holy Trinity
Church Rectory, Southwick
by Rev Robert Dixon – Rector of Holy Trinity Church 32

1930s Scrapbook 34

The Loyal Order of Ancient Shepherds
Friendly Society. Pride of Southwick Lodge
by Arthur Turnbull 38

Southwick and the Second World War 41

Memories of Evacuation by Jim Weatherill 44

The Southwick Mafia by John Curtis 63

Suddick Roots and Childhood Memories 73

Southwick Shipyard's Last Days 89

Memories of Pickersgill's by Leslie Tate 95

Pictures of Recent Years 98

Timber Beach
by Paul Mortimer – Durham Wildlife Trust 100

List of Subscribers 103

High Southwick

# Foreword

Peter Gibson's fourth book on Southwick is even more of a ragbag than those that came before; and a wonderful ragbag it is. It includes some remarkable social history, cleverly concocted from a judicious blend of the pages of local newspapers with the memories of friends. Have you ever read a more vivid and moving account of the home front in the Second World War? Have you ever known a community so skilfully depicted, or an author with such a deft human touch?

Peter's history has now reached modern times. That means he plays a part in the story himself. Before he settles down to tell from the inside how life was for Southwick's young tearaways of the '50s and '60s, he outlines the story of his ancestors. Six generations of Southwick Gibsons have grown up in that inflated, industrial village, and have changed as it did. Now, though Southwick has sadly lost its historic purpose and may be losing its identity, we can be thankful that Southwick will never vanish altogether while Peter's book is there to be read.

Tom Corfe, October 1996

First Published by Southwick Publications in December 1996

Copyright © Peter Gibson 1996

ISBN 0-9513908-3-X

Design and Presentation by Alan Brett and Peter Gibson

Typesetting by Harry Clark and Andrew Clark

Produced by Rufus Abajas

The line drawings in the chapter 'Suddick Roots and Childhood Memories', and the shipyard characters on page 92 and 93 have been created by Pal Palmer from information and memories supplied by the author. The copyright for the drawings belongs to Pal Palmer © 1996.

## AN ORIGINAL SONG,

BY THE LATE R. HODGSON, MILL INN, SOUTHWICK.

## "Canny Auld Suddick."

AIR—" The Braes of Gleniffer."

By Trent's stream, ere the twilight had faded,
   Alone and dejected, an exile did roam—
The flowers on its banks shed their beauties unheeded,
   For his thoughts were afar on his own native home.
He thought of old Suddick, the place of his childhood,
   Where barefoot he waded on *Wear's* muddy shore,
Or gathered the sloes that grew in the wildwood,
   And sigh'd as he thought he might ne'er see them more.

He thought of the Pond where to water the horses,
   He'd hie when the *horn* off to fodder would call ;
He thought of the spot where youth mustered its forces
   'Neath the ivy that hung o'er the *Boarding School Wall*—
He thought of the *Green* where a youngster he sported
   Till the last light would gleam from the old *Smithy* door,
And the Cot where sweet slumber his eylids first courted—
   And sighed as he thought he might ne'er see them more.

In fancy he saw the old moss-covered *Quarries*,
   Where *Trencher Tree* stood on the top of the *Hill*,
And the old *Marleypots* where he gathered blackberries,
   And listened the clack of the old *Wooden Mill*.
In fancy he saw the *Nursery Trees* waving,
   And remembered that one his initials bore ;
Then saw the *Well Dene* with its modest stream laving,
   And sigh'd as he thought he might ne'er see them more.

But folly it is to be sad and downhearted,
   None knows the blessing a day may bring forth—
Scarce from his mind had the vision departed,
   Ere he traversed again his first home in the north.
He's left the sweet *Trent*, with its green hills and valleys.
   And mingles again with his cronies of yore ;
In the midst of old scenes, oft delighted he dallies,
   As in freedom and peace he enjoys them once more.

# Farming Lives

*Harry Bruce (aged 90) was from Carley Place and he worked on Carley Hill Farm which was leased by the Moss family. Here he met Ann Moss (aged 84) whom he married in 1934. In an interview on February 8th 1996 Mr and Mrs Bruce recalled some of their farming life:-*

It was hard work on the farm in those days but there were many pleasant sunny days and it was a healthy life. Carley Hill Farm was fairly large and the land was rented from Lady Stafford and the Wearmouth Coal Company. Ann's grandfather had started the farm last century. The family came from Cumbria and farmed Field House Farm at Boldon before settling at Carley Hill.

One incident stands out in our memory. In 1926 two cows bought from Sunderland Cattle Mart infected the dairy herd with Foot and Mouth Disease. Forty cows had to be slaughtered. A large pit was dug in the quarry and after the beasts were shot their carcasses were burnt and buried. It was a sad time seeing so many animals killed and it was a terrible blow to the family's livelihood. There was no compensation in those days. We can remember a trough of disinfectant where people entering and leaving the farm dipped the soles of their shoes.

The Moss family hired Southwick Red House Farm from Lady Stafford of Sussex and we went to live and work there after we were married in 1934. Clifford's had previously occupied the farmhouse which was situated on the site where the factory which was called Hepworth and Grandage now stands, and over the road to the Aged Miners' Homes in North Hylton Road. The farmhouse was the last house in Southwick and it was in the country. Rabbits ran to and fro across the road and there were pheasants in the fields. We farmed the land and kept pigs, ducks, geese and hens. But there was always the threat of foxes taking our poultry. We didn't have cattle but it was a welcome rest for Ann who had worked long hours on the dairy farm at Carley Hill.

Lady Stafford's son inherited Southwick Red House Farmlands, and after the war Harry showed him the land and the boundaries of the farm. At the extreme western boundary at the Road Ends we could look down at the left hand side into Swallow Dene. It was a beautiful place where annual Sunday School treats were held. We spent a lot of time there with our children where we had picnics. It was well named because swallows would swoop down above our heads. From the 'Low Road' miners on their way to Hylton Colliery from Southwick and people out on walks could look down into the Dene. Later, it was filled in and factories are on the site today. During our walk Mr Stafford was fascinated to learn

*Frank and Emma Clifford were tenants on Southwick Red House Farm from c. 1920 to c. 1928. Their children, Violet and Kenneth, attended Todd's private school on The Green during the 1920s.*

that part of the farm at the riverside had been owned by his family, but was sold or leased to Swan Hunters' to build concrete ships.

During the war old Mr Moss was growing weak. From his bed he asked Harry to go and bring him some wheat from each field on Carley Hill Farm. Harry took our boy Gordon with him and placed samples of wheat in separate bags, and took them to him as requested. He died not long afterwards. The

*Looking east in the 1920s and showing the original Red House farmhouse on the right. On the left is the Stackyard and the farmhouse.*

farm was left to his third son, Jimmy. In 1954 Jimmy Moss was accidentally killed in a shooting accident on the farm. His widow married Alfie Maw. In the 1960s the Maws left Carley Hill Farm and it was demolished during the development of Carley Hill Estate. In about 1963-64 we came off Southwick Red House Farm and it was demolished to build Hepworth and Grandage factory.

*The Moss family in about 1922. Left to right: Billy, Bob (on mother's knee), Mrs Angelina Moss, Mr James Moss, Ann (in front of father), Jim (seated), Tom, old aunt Elizabeth holding baby Lizzie, Angelina.*

*Ann Moss feeding hens in the farmyard - Early 1930s. The white building housed what was known as the top byre.*

*Carley Hill Farmhouse in about 1900. The front entrance (pictured above) was rarely used, recalls Mrs Bruce. Everything happened at the rear entrance in the farmyard. The farmhouse was later faced with cement.*

Haytime on Moss' Farm in 1929. It was first cut green and left to dry in the sun. The hay was turned over to allow the other side to dry. Pikes of hay were made in the hayfield. Extra workers were employed for haytime in June and July. The photograph shows workers resting against pikes of hay at teatime. Tea was taken into the fields for the workers. Nowadays the hay is baled by a field baling machine.

Making Haystacks in 1930.
A horse drawn bogie (pictured right) was used to transport the pikes of hay from the fields to the stackyard. The horse was backed up until the edge of the tilted bogie went under the pike. The rope attached to a roller at the front of the bogie (seen right) was positioned around the pike, and the handle of the roller turned to pull the pike onto the bogie which was almost levelled. The horse was led to the stackyard and the bogie positioned near to the haystack under construction and tilted. A hay fork was used to firmly hold the pike while the horse was led away leaving the pike on the ground.
Right - At this stage of construction the hay could be thrown up with hay forks.

When the stack became too high to work from the ground a hay pole (seen in centre of photograph) was used to lift the pikes. The hay pole was portable and held vertically in position by four strong ropes which were secured to the ground by four large pins. A large fork-like implement on the end of a wire rope was pressed into the pike of hay. The wire rope was attached to a horse (out of picture) via a pulley at the top of the hay pole. The horse was led away and the pike hoisted

to the top of the haystack as shown in the photograph. Here the 'Stacker' took over and delegated the work of placing the hay at suitable places with the hay forks.

Depending on the circumstances the hay was used for 'Winter keep' or sold by the farm. 'Hay Well Won' was often advertised in the local press.

Stackyard and bottom cow byre in 1930. In the foreground is 'Damsel' and her foal. On the left is an embankment where marley stone was dug out and used for filling holes in farm roadways.

Farm employee Sidney Shield with the horse 'Dick' and milk float carrying a churn (in 1931). The farm delivered milk to customers in Southwick, Fulwell and Monkwearmouth. The inscription - "Jas Moss Carley Hill Farm" is above the wheel.

Joe Henderson, who lived next door to the Bruce's on Southwick Red House Farm, is pictured 'scuffling' (harrowing) in the early 1930s. A frame with iron teeth was pulled by a horse between the rows of potatoes to loosen the earth and remove weeds at the same time. Afterwards on 'earthing up' or 'rowing up' plough was employed to raise up the soil on the potato crop. Southwick Red House Farm took over Linge's Market Garden in the early 1940s. Burntland Avenue can be seen in the background.

*Right: Jim McVay is pictured with foxes shot on Carley Hill Farm by Jimmy Moss in about 1950. "The foxes made their home in the corn", recalled Harry Bruce. "We knew they were there and Jimmy took his shotgun with him when he cut the corn. The wheat was cut at the base by an old fashioned binder before the days of the combined harvester. The binder was horse drawn and as it made its way through the field foxes darted out. Jimmy stood up in the seat and shot them." Jim McVay worked for the Carters of Carley Lodge.*

*St Columba's football team in 1932-33 season which played in the Church Institute League. Harry Bruce – middle of front row. Other Southwick characters are: Front row on the right – Tommy Evans, and Billy Evans – middle row third from left (see page 67). Goalkeeper standing is Jack Washington (see also page 27).*

*Ann and Harry Bruce outlived their two children Gordon and Jean. Gordon is pictured with West Southwick class of about 1946, back row fourth from our right. He died of meningitis not long after this photograph was taken. Jean Bruce died in 1995 aged 59.*

*1921 aerial view of the shipyards and showing nearby farmland. The railway embankment separates the shipyards from the rest of Southwick. North Hylton Road is seen leading across the top of the photograph to Southwick Redhouse farmhouse (top centre). Swallow Dene is top left. Observe, the large number of ships on the berths and in the river.*

*Happy days! Harry and Ann Bruce and daughter Jean prior to the war. "Swallow Dene was a beautiful place," said Mr Bruce, "where we spent many happy times".*

*The rear of Southwick Red House Farm in 1948. Pictured are friends of the Bruce family.*

Ann Bruce died peacefully in hospital in September 1996.

# The 1870s:
# I. Some Developments and the Local Boards

In the year 1800 and thereabouts a group of the leading citizens of Southwick met once per year in a public house in the village for the management of the Board of Highways. The Nuisance Removal Act had been adopted at about this time but it did not work very well. When Southwick Local Board of Health was established in 1863 it was apparently such an insignificant event that it was not recorded in the local press. Nonetheless the forming of Southwick's own government was a major step in the development of the rapidly growing village where incredible changes were taking place. The Local Board inherited many problems and the first few years were particularly hard. William Dodd Pratt, the local builder and brick and tile manufacturer, was the first chairman from 1863 to 1867; and he soon led an efficient and well organised Southwick Local Board. Despite the many problems they had to face, they had strong local support because the community was united to face the threat from Sunderland.

In December 1866 there was a public meeting of about seventy ratepayers to oppose the proposed Parliamentary legislation brought by Sunderland to absorb the village. Anthony Scott from the pottery was one of the oldest inhabitants of the village and he reflected on the deep feeling for Southwick. "... For if they had not been born with Southwick, they had grown with its growth, shared its trials, borne the burden of its battles, and had raised its government from a parish meeting to a well constituted Board of Health ... They had fought three

battles with the Corporation and had come off victorious and were prepared to fight the fourth."

The Local Board of Health was concerned with the problems which resulted from the rapid growth of industry and housing. Sanitary problems had been caused by the erection of houses to the south of the village green in Waterloo Place and Stafford Street in 1818 without adequate building regulations. Similarly, houses at Low Southwick on the bankside were built in the 1830s and 1840s without sewers, drains, paving or water supply. In the 1840s heavy rain caused torrents to flow freely down the streets and took with it human and animal excrement, urine, refuse thrown from houses, as well as some of the rubbish and filth which filled the back lanes and made them almost impassible. At Cross Street at the centre of Low Southwick the mixture settled into a large pool of stagnant and stinking sludge. Nearby was a privately owned pump which served a well used by the locals. Cases of fever had been reported in the neighbourhood and almost every house had a tank which caught fresh drinking water that fell as rain as an alternative to the well.

In May 1846 The Sunderland and Durham County Herald called for the cleaning up of Low Southwick but landlords did nothing. Working men found it necessary to live near to industry but were anxious to stay healthy for work. In March 1848 The Southwick Working Mens' Health Association was formed at a well attended meeting in the National School. Workers called upon

landlords to clear and clean the streets where disease could fester. One man stated that owing to the lack of basic amenities like paving, sewers and drains " ... civilised life exists in primeval rudeness and unreclaimed disorder!"

Money was raised by public subscription to install gas lighting in August 1854. Lamp-posts were erected at intervals from the eastern boundary in Southwick Lane near the Halfway House through to the village and down Stoney Lane, and west up the New Road (later Crown Road) to the Glass Houses. On his first visit the much awaited lamplighter was followed by numerous youngsters and adults who enthusiastically cheered when each lamp was lit. Shortly afterwards pipes were laid to light 'The Low Road' - a dangerous thoroughfare from the Halfway House, crossing the waggonway and through the fields to Low Southwick. And on Sunday evening November 19th 1854 Holy Trinity Church " ... appeared for the first time in all the splendour of gas light." Reported the *Sunderland News*.

During the 1850s and 1860s notable buildings were erected: The Ebenezer Independent Chapel (1854), Wandlass Place, High Southwick; Clockwell Street Primitive Methodist Chapel (1859), (architect W.D.Pratt prepared the plans free of charge); Durham Constabulary Police Station (1865), Stoney Lane; United Methodist Free Church and Schools (1867), King Street, Low Southwick, (architect John Tillman); Weslyan Methodist Chapel (1868), Town Street (later the Green), (architect John Tillman). During the latter part of 1869 a new main road which linked Southwick Lane near The Halfway House to Stoney Lane (opposite Clockwell Street) resulted in a direct route from the Wheatsheaf to the Alexandra Institute (1867), which was the principal building in Southwick.

The population of Southwick increased from 2,721 in 1851 to 4,263 in 1861, and increased again to 6,566 by 1871. At the beginning of the new decade of the 1870s Southwick was on the eve of some great developments. Kelly's 1873 Directory describes the two villages - "Part of High Southwick is very old and the houses bear evident proof of its antiquity. Low Southwick is more modern and is the seat of business, having shipbuilding yards, glass works (bottle and sheet), limeworks, earthenware, brick and tile manufacturers, and engine factory. Iron shipbuilding is beginning to be carried on extensively, while wooden shipbuilding has almost ceased... The landowners are Capt. Stafford, W.D.Pratt Esq.., James Herring Esq.., Anthony Scott Esq.., G.Hudson Esq.., the Rector of Southwick."

Southwick was isolated in the 1860s, and the inhabited area was relatively small when compared to the extensive farmlands and quarries which surrounded the built up area within the township's boundaries. Southwick was surveyed in 1868 (the 1868 map is in Sunderland Museum) immediately prior to much needed and extensive housing development on the Well Dene Field Estate at West Southwick; the Hill View Estate where most of the streets were named after poets; and on the Town End Field Estate where Armitage, Barnett and others built Morgan Street and James Armitage Street

etc. By 1872 Cornhill Estate was progressing when Kertch Street, Varna Street, Bow Street and houses in Southwick Lane had been built. The 1872 map shows two rows of cottages at Pleasant Row on Fulwell Road, Carley Place; as well as dwellings in Mary Street at West Southwick.

Southwick was linked to Monkwearmouth village by the ancient thoroughfare Southwick Lane, which was bordered by Monkwearmouth Colliery on one side and fields on the other. By 1872 the fields were filled with houses when Sunderland's development spread west towards Southwick's borders. Warwick Street and Devonshire Street to Bond Street and Albany Street were followed by Finsbury Street, Chilton Street, Byron Street and others by the end of the 1870s. The Borough housing was separated from Cornhill at Southwick by what became known as Farm Street.

Early in 1870 Southwick Local Board of Health comprised Robert Thompson, shipbuilder (Chairman), Thomas Gowdy, managing partner of the Crown Bottleworks, John Crown the shipbuilder, John T.Todd, butcher, James Herring, gentleman landowner, Messrs. W.D.Pratt, Anderson and Grey, and the Sunderland based architect George Andrew Middlemiss. The surveyor and inspector of nuisances was John Cook. The Board met monthly and there were two main committees: The Finance Committee and The Buildings, Highways and Sewerage Committee. The district rate was one shilling (5p) in the pound and the rateable value was £11,500. The Board had the responsibility and power to determine the development and layout of a new model village and enforced bye-laws to prevent

previous sanitary mistakes recurring.

The Local Board answered to The Southwick Ratepayers Association who were a large and influential pressure group that monitored decisions made by the Board. For example, in April 1873, a rate was levied at 1s 2d (6p) in the pound. However, owing to rising costs of stone for highways the rate was changed to 1s 6d (8p) in the pound. At a large meeting of the Ratepayers Association in the Alexandra Institute the Board was severely censured " ... for their reckless extravagance." The rate was changed again to 1s 2d in the pound.

The Chairman's post was a difficult and time-consuming position. In April 1871 Robert Thompson was not returned at the poll. His successor as Chairman, George A.Middlemiss suffered the same fate the following year. Despite Robert Thompson regaining a seat on the Board in October 1871 when Edward Anderson's seat became available, all of the Board's nine members declined to stand as Chairman in April 1872. An extraordinary situation arose when James Herring was elected Chairman by six votes to two but refused to take the seat, even though his colleagues had offered their help and support. While the monthly meeting in April 1872 continued James Herring left the Board Room and sat alone in another room. He was called to take his seat as Chairman at the table but remained silent. The Board shut up shop and went home before the business was completed. However, at the next monthly meeting James Herring took the chair without comment.

Despite building developments on several estates, houses could not be built quickly enough, and the township became overcrowded by the influx of new workers for the Hylton, Southwick and Monkwearmouth Railway, the iron foundry and other industrial developments taking place in the rising manufacturing district. In one place a coalhouse had been converted to a bedroom and in June 1872 the Board issued caution bills to landlords under the Lodging Housing Act. The demand for workmens' houses in Southwick forced up the value of property.

Work on the new railway which divided the Southwicks began in March 1872 and one hundred men were initially employed on the scheme. When completed the railway was expected to enhance the trade and resources and attract more industry and commerce to Southwick. There was cheaper transit of completed products for the home market and Southwick Goods Station was a new facility to receive raw materials.

Robert Thompson Junior

*Robert Thompson Junior, the successful Southwick shipbuilder of Carley Lodge was a powerful man and a good leader. He was Chairman of Southwick Local Board during the 1870s for three separate periods, i.e. 1870-71, 1874-77 and again in 1879 when the retiring Chairman – John*

*Taylor Todd – proposed Robert Thompson as his successor. He was a straight man with high standards and ideals, and he worked hard for Southwick. In April 1876 when he was thanked by the Local Board for his ability to manage the Board's affairs, and for his courtesy to other Board members he said: "I have always endeavoured to do my duty and I am glad my efforts are appreciated by the Board."*

*Robert Thompson was an active member of Southwick Liberal Party. He had gained respect on Wearside and in January 1880 the Rev Collingwood tried to persuade him to become Chairman of Southwick School Board. Mr Collingwood said, "He was a gentleman who would sustain the dignity of the Board and would make it generally respected." Robert Thompson declined the position because he didn't have the time to carry out the Chairman's duties.*

In 1872 George S.Gulston laid out a new yard for iron shipbuilding. In November 1874 a 'Great Fire' broke out at 8.30 p.m. at the yard which was situated at an isolated spot west of the Ballast Hill. It was

reported that not a drop of water could be obtained to subdue the fire because there was not a hydrant nearby and the hose was too short. The wood offices were allowed to burn itself out, although the police and workmen led by Sergt. Collins saved the ship on the berth which was ready to be launched. In July 1876 Gulstons launched a steam ferryboat to ply between Bodlewell Lane and Monkwearmouth Shore, and to carry a maximum of fiftyfive passengers. In the same month the yard was put up for sale by auction. The little known John Priestman eventually opened out the yard again in January 1882.

Meanwhile, Southwick Local Board ordered the owners of buildings in private streets to level, pave, flag, channel and kerb the streets and footpaths adjoining their property. The owners were given a period of time to complete the work

and when it elapsed the Board carried out the work by first advertising for tenders. The Board then billed the property owners and some were reluctant to pay. There was dispute over defining public and private roads. The 1737 map (see Volume 1 p6) shows one main highway from Monkwearmouth which passed through the village green and forked to Bowdon (Boldon) and Newcastle. The only other road in Southwick was Scotts Bank which led from the ferry landing (previously a ford existed there) to join the main highway on the green. Scotts Bank was said to have derived its name from the Scottish Army which had taken Sunderland for Parliament and passed by that way in 1644 to engage in skirmishes at Downhill with the Royalists who had come out of Newcastle. Alternatively, the thoroughfare was said to have taken its name from Scott's Pottery, which is perhaps the most accurate explanation. These ancient roads will have been maintained for centuries by the parish and were subsequently classified as public roads. Another thoroughfare – Stoney Lane – however, had been originally created for the 18th century lime trade. When it fell into disuse it still served the purpose of access between High and Low Southwick, and it too was maintained by the parish. In 1870 it was judged a public road and the County Court ordered the Local Board to pay for street and footpath improvements adjoining the houses which had been built either side of the old wagonway in Albert Row and Stoney Lane. The decision was a major set-back for the Board. The large scale building of dwellings on the new estates developed into new private streets and the owners, particularly in the vicinity of Stoney Lane, refused to pay for street improvements, and the Board summonsed non payers.

In these early years of Southwick's government there were disputes with landowners regarding rights of way, and Southwick Local Board attempted to enforce its authority during the 1870s to protect the interests of the villagers. Ancient deeds and documents had either been lost, or were vague, or did not mention rights of way which were exercised by the villagers. Some rights of way had been passed down the ages by word of mouth and tradition, whereas others were developed during the industrial growth.

In mid 1870 the Board enforced the opening up of the top of Stoney Lane which had been blocked up. But in June 1870 landowner Captain Stafford erected a gate to block the road to the ferry

at Southwick Beach. The road was entered at the bottom of Collin Place and Adelaide Street, and can be clearly seen on the 1851 map (see Southwick on Wear Vol. 1 p33), leading to the ferry near to several shipyards. The ferry was an important facility and an estimated five hundred persons used it every day. The Local Board claimed a public right of way which was from before living memory. Captain Stafford, however, maintained that he could prove the ferry plied with his permission and the ferry owners paid a fee for the privilege. Members of the Board visited the site and George A.Middlemiss wanted to smash down the gate, but there was no seconder. The blocking up of the ferry road probably had something to do with the sale of six acres of land from Stafford to Clark who was bringing his engine building business to Southwick.

George Clark was a potential large employer and ratepayer and the Local Board desired him to come to Southwick. The members did not want to prejudice the chances of losing the engineering works and made their feelings known at a well attended public meeting in February 1871 in the Alexandra Institute to discuss the public right of way to the ferry landing. George Clark needed the removal of the ferry to build his works and offered the village a fifteen feet wide road further up river and next to his proposed works. The new site for the ferry and road was accepted. By 1874 Clark's was capable of employing between 900 and 1000 hands.

Another great difference of opinion arose in May 1874, this time between the Board and Matteson's Crown Glassworks. Matteson's claimed they had opened the private road at the end

of Crown Road which passed through the Glassworks and to the Ballast Hill for the convenience of their shipyard tenants and access to houses on the Ballast Hill. Southwick Local Board, however, claimed a public right of way on behalf of the villagers when Matteson's blocked up the road. During a Board meeting James Herring angrily moved that the surveyor should go with a hammer and knock down the paling. The motion was not seconded. The Board chose to write to Matteson's and warned them that if they did not remove the obstruction the Board would pull it down. John Matteson "dared" the Board to do what it liked! Matteson had called the Board's bluff; they could not do anything about it and the road remained closed.

The most important right of way case in the History of Southwick was the Well Field question. The field, situated to the south and south west of Holy Trinity Church, is marked on early maps under various names - In 1746 'Great Well Dene Field', 1851 'Well Dene Field'; 1868 'Bleach Yard'. The villagers had enjoyed an ancient right of way to collect water from the wells, to water their livestock and use of the field as a drying and bleaching ground.

The field belonged to the Grey family from 1630, and in 1808/10 Thomas Brunton took it over. Dorothy Grey was said to have given the people of Southwick "… full, perfect and legal right to bleach calico and clothes, and use the water unlimited …" But Brunton had occasionally tried to stop the practice. In about 1847 Anthony Scott, the potter, was summoned to court for sending his servant to dry clothes on the Well Field, which Anthony Scott had considered a right. The case was dismissed. On

*Snow covered Well Field early in 1987. Although prefabs were built on the field after the war and stood for about ten years, the Well Field reverted to an open space again. The people of Southwick still have a right of way today which was challenged and won in court in 1877.*

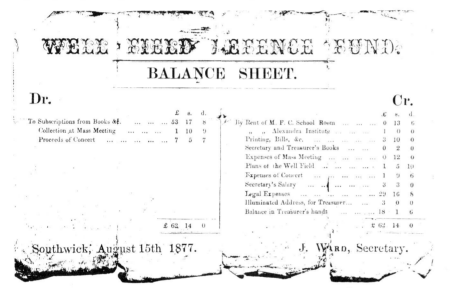

*Well Field Defence Fund balance sheet which demonstrates the resolve of the people to preserve their right of way, and resist the Pratt family taking over the Well Field.*

another occasion Brunton saw some clothes drying on the field and rode over with the intention of stopping it . But when he got there he found that the clothes were his own!

Thomas Pratt bought the field in 1858 and it was developed with the surrounding land for building purposes. The dene at the west end of the Well Field, which consisted of a deep valley and plantation, was filled and levelled. The pond used to water villager's cattle was drained and levelled and two of the three wells had been covered. By 1866 Thomas Pratt had built four cottages at the east end of the field and he intended to cover all of it with dwellings .

There was concern among the people of Southwick over these developments. The public right of way to the Well Field was brought up and then dropped again in March 1870, when there were suspicions that Thomas Pratt intended to fill in the last remaining well, which was considered useful when water was off in the village. And, again in August 1872 when a petition signed by 88 ratepayers and inhabitants  of Southwick was handed to the Board to request "... The Local Board of Southwick to open out the old wells in the Well Field as they were formerly, and to erect a drinking fountain for the

public; and also a pond for the cattle and furthermore prevent obstruction of the bleaching yard." The Board took action and instructed the surveyor to open the old well on the south of the Well Field and test the water; and to repair the well on the north end of the Well Field. However, while carrying out the work the surveyor was approached by W.D.Pratt (who was also a member of the Board) who ordered him and his workmen off his father's land.

There was widespread ill-feeling in Southwick about the rights of the Well Field and in March 1877 the patience of four Southwick men ran out when they took drastic steps to open up the right of way. Joseph Williams, Christopher Philliskirk, Christopher Thompson and Thomas Turnbull ended up in court when they tore and saw down a fence on the Well Field at Southwick, on March 5th at 11.30 pm, which belonged to Thomas Pratt. The four men had tremendous support for their actions from the people of Southwick, and several old inhabitants of the village gave evidence of the rights of way to the Well Field within living memory. There was great interest in the case and many people from Southwick were in court to hear the verdict of the Bench: That the four men had a perfect right to do what they did, and the fence was an obstruction which they were justified to remove.

The Pratt family were not happy with the decision of the Bench and decided to take 'The Great Southwick Case', as it became known, for trial at Durham Assizes.

The people of Southwick organised an association to defend the right of way on the Well Field, and to defend the four men who pulled the fence down in the interests of the public rights. On June 21st 1877 a parade of villagers followed a brass band and a banner which read: "Southwick - popular right not privilege" noisily passed through the streets of the village. A crowd of about 800 people assembled near the Well Field for a mass meeting to hear speakers who produced more evidence of their rights. A statement was read out that had been written by the late Joseph Wandless who had been an estate owner at Southwick, dated January 1871: "I remember in 1792, which was a dry summer, being sent by my father, who was a farmer at Fulwell, with some cows and the old black bull to the well at Southwick. When there I went a birdnesting in the dene, and the old black bull tore up an old woman's sheet which was lying on the field to dry, and for which I received 'a good hammering'. I also went to the Well Field for water to take to the harvest field.

"In 1830 at the parish meeting held at Southwick certain documents were brought forward which proved that the public had legal rights in the Well Field and I read them over and over again ..."

In July 1877 the Local Board came to an agreement with Thomas Pratt to divide the land. It was agreed that the Local Board's part be not used for any other than public purposes or for erecting public buildings. The Pratts dropped the charges against the four men. Despite the fact the Well Field Defence Committee did not at first recognise the agreement between Thomas Pratt and the Local Board, the authority erected railings around the public's part and laid out the field.

When W.D.Pratt put up for re-election to the Local Board in April 1879 he was not returned at the poll. Pratt's opponents had issued handbills to point out his "antagonistic" attitude to the interests of the ratepayers on the

Well Field question, and sewerage and tramway schemes. Furthermore, at another triennial election in December 1879 William Dodd Pratt lost his seat on the Southwick School Board. He had been chairman for the previous three years and his loss was a serious blow to the School Board. His building knowledge had been of great value during the erection of the Southwick Board Schools, and his hard work and regular attendance at meetings had earned respect among his colleagues on the School Board.

Meanwhile, the Local Board were concerned to develop the facilities of the growing village. Nonetheless, it was difficult for the authority to keep pace with improvements at the speed at which houses were being built. In fact many were becoming inhabited out of sheer necessity before the surveyor could inspect them and issue a certificate which passed them as habitable.

In 1870 Southwick was linked to the national telegraph system and later the postal arrangements were improved following complaints that businesses were losing money owing to the late delivery of mail; and furthermore a post box was positioned at Cornhill Estate and one on the green, to save the inhabitants the long trek to the post office at Low Southwick.

The rateable value increased from £11,500 in 1870 to £15,800 in 1874, and again to £18,000 by 1878 which increased the Local Board's power of borrowing. A water cart had been purchased in 1872 to wash down the streets which became very dusty during the summer months, and blinding on windy days. Loans were secured to undertake important drainage and sewerage works at Carley Place

where the land lay low and stagnant water gathered which gave rise to the fear of the outbreak of pestilence. Once again dwellings were being built faster than drainage schemes. On the Town End Field estate it was reported that householders threw waste water into backyards and back lanes. The high mortality rate at Southwick in August 1878 was blamed on undrained estates by some members of the Local Board. John Crown, however, blamed the overcrowding at Low Southwick which was seconded by W.D.Pratt who stated "... the overcrowding in the lower parts of the town was horrible. People, it seemed, had come out of better houses and gone into smaller ones where they would have to pay less rent."

The rapid increase of population had necessitated more stringent measures to protect the health of the villagers. The 1872 Public Health Act enforced the Local Board to advertise for a part-time Medical Officer of Health and Sanitary Inspector. There was loud laughter at a Board meeting in January 1874 when Mr Hodgson commented that " ... it had been said at the pantomime at the Theatre Royal that Southwick Local Board wanted a Medical Officer for £10 per year. It seems that the doctors had not been at the pantomime or we would have had applications." There were only two applications for the post and Dr. R.Ayre-Smith was appointed in February 1874. He would work hard for his salary of £10 per annum.

Southwick street lamps were fuelled by gas supplied by the Sunderland Gas Company at a rate of £3-10s (£3.50) per lamp. The lamps were lit over the period from August 5th to May 20th; except at the full moon when every other lamp was unlit for three nights. The lamps were not lit at all during the summer months. The Board entered into annual contracts and when the Gas Company put up the price of gas in the summer of 1873 the two sides failed to agree, and Southwick streets were in darkness for two months during the autumn of 1873. 'Fair Play' wrote to the *Sunderland Times* and warned of burglaries and garrottings (robbery with violence) in the darkness. Fair Play accused the Local Board of forcing the hand of ratepayers to buy shares in the proposed new Southwick Gas Company. Afterwards a new contract with Sunderland Gas Company was signed and Southwick streets were lit again.

The 1870 Education Act provided education for all children, but it was not until November 1873 that the ratepayers of Southwick, fearing government intervention which might have allowed in their 'enemy' Sunderland, met in the Alexandra Institute for the purpose of forming Southwick School Board.

Party politics and religious issues were involved during the build up to the elections which took place in January 1874, and was organised by Sunderland Board of Guardians. The first Southwick School Board comprised: William J. Clark (engine builder); James Herring (Southwick gentleman); John B. King (glassmaker and working men's candidate); Rev. C.S. Collingwood (Rector); John W. Matteson (glass manufacturer); James Armitage (builder); George McAndrew (shipwright, Roman Catholic and working men's candidate).

The first meeting took place in March 1874 in the offices of the Local Board though it was agreed to take temporary offices in Robert Hodgson's house at High Southwick until a school was built.

There was much to do and the Rev. C.S. Collingwood was voted as chairman; a Finance Committee and General Purpose Committee were appointed; standing orders, regulations and bye-laws had to be written; and the priority was to take a census of Southwick children to determine the number of places for the proposed new schools. It was found that there were about 250 children attending the National School. 156 children attending private schools in Sunderland where a better education was available for children belonging to parents from the 'middle and upper working classes'. A number of miners' children attended the Colliery School which was provided by the Colliery owners 'for that class of children'. 234 children attended several private schools in Southwick and 363 children did not attend any school whatsoever!

At that time anyone could establish a school and the School Board sent out inspectors to report on accommodation and education at the private schools in the neighbourhood. Three of them were found to be in a 'wretched condition'.

The School Board were concerned about the large number of Southwick children running wild on the streets and a School Site and Building Committee was formed. Its first task was to bring the children together in a temporary school at the Alexandra Institute. However, the idea was abandoned in January 1875 because of inadequate conveniences. There was no other suitable accommodation in the township and Southwick School Board was forced to patiently wait until new schools were built.

A piece of land was bought from Col. Stafford at the corner of back High Southwick and Fulwell Road at the cost of 4 shillings (20p) per square yard. It was decided to build a school for 680 pupils and provision was made for extensions. High Southwick Board Schools would consist of three schools - Boys, Girls and Infants. The architect was Martin Greener and William Davison won the contract in June 1876 to build the schools for £5,352 and a little under £8,000 was borrowed, to be repayed over a period of fifty years. Mr. R. Hodgson was appointed Clerk of Works. In those early days of the School Board they reserved the right, in circumstances of family hardship, to exempt from school children who were required to work to maintain the upkeep of their family.

The School Board thought that a practical man with a knowledge of buildings was needed as Chairman to monitor the progress of the schools which were under construction, and W. D. Pratt was elected Chairman in January 1877 for a term of three years. The retiring chairman, Rev. C. S. Collingwood seemed happy with the decision and became Vice-Chairman. In his opening speech W. D. Pratt said: "I have no other object in view of coming to the Board but the benefit of Southwick. If I had consulted my own feelings and inclinations I should not have come out as a member, but would have spent my time at home. Seeing, however, the need for education in that place, and seeing that Southwick was far behind other places in the educational facilities it afforded for children and the number of children that were running wild in the streets, I think it is necessary that everyone should buckle to and make Southwick equal to other places in this respect."

The new Education Act of 1876 gave the School Board more power over parents and employers of children and it brought into force the principle of 'indirect compulsion'. The School Board preferred, however, 'moral persuasion' before taking cases of non-attendance to the magistrates.

In July 1877 the School Board became aware of serious discrepancies between the actual work done on the new schools and the specifications. Walls were not the required thickness; there was no concrete foundations for the boundary wall; window frames were made of lighter thickness wood and windows were glazed with inferior glass. On top of this inferior workmanship was criticised by the School Board. The Clerk of Works had resigned and William Davison, the builder, went bankrupt and couldn't complete the work. Because of his insolvency he had to resign his seat on Southwick Local Board of Health. William Davison later recovered from his bankruptcy and became a successful Southwick builder.

New tenders were invited to finish the schools and the architect promised that defective work would be replaced.

Despite the subsequent delay of opening the school, scheduled for mid August 1877, the Rev. Collingwood brought, what he considered to be, the most important question before the School Board at a meeting in October 1877 - the religious education of the children. He moved "That the Board Schools at

*The Rev. C.S. Collingwood was Rector at Southwick from 1863 to 1898.*

Southwick open each morning and close each evening with prayer, and that a lesson in Scripture be given daily." Mr King pointed out that "the children of many persuasions would attend the school, and some with no persuasion at all." And it was felt by other members of the School Board that religious education should be free from sectarianism. A resolution passed by the School Board stated that the school will open and close with the Lord's Prayer, and Scriptures read out without comment. The Rev. Collingwood said he was 'shocked' by the decision of the Board.

The schools eventually opened in November 1877 and the fees were fixed as follows: Boys and girls under 7 years, twopence per week; boys aged 7 and upwards, fourpence per week; girls aged 7 and upwards, threepence per week; and when three children of the same family attended school the third child would not be charged.

Despite the major achievement of providing schools for all Southwick children the School Board anticipated problems of persuading and educating parents to send their children regularly to school. Compulsion like this had not been known before and the school fees became a strain on some family budgets. A full-time truant officer was appointed and in January 1878 seventytwo cases of non-attendance at school were brought before a committee made up of the whole School Board. The truant officer served another fifty notices. The poverty in Southwick at this period was recorded at the committee meeting when it was revealed that the main reason for non-attendance of children was because they had no shoes or stockings to wear. And a number of parents were excused the non-attendance of their children

because they were unable to pay the fees.

A visiting committee had been formed and the truant officer reported in January 1878 "…visited a house in Back Wear Street last week in which Michael Clark and a man of the name of Foster live together with their children. There is not a woman nor an article of furniture in the house, not even a bed to lie upon that I could see. The poverty and squalor which exists is appalling. The children in their present dirty condition ought not to be allowed to enter school where children are clean …" Further, it was reported in April 1878 that when the truant officer visited the homes of children with arrears of school fees, he learned that their fathers had been unemployed for several weeks.

In June 1878, when thirty more families appeared before the Board Committee, free passes were issued to children when severe hardship was proved by parents. The action of the School Board was having the desired effect when there was a large increase of scholars attending school. In April 1878 it was recorded that 561 attended out of 636 on the register; and by October 1878, 667 children regularly attended the Board School. Some parents, however, would not send their children to school and were summoned before the Magistrates in the hope that it would "act as a terror" to others.

By the late 1870s there is more evidence of a recession of trade. At a School Board meeting in September 1878 it was stated that the " … small amount got in the shape of school fees was due to the large amount of destitution prevalent in the township."

Southwick School Board member, the shipbuilder Robert Thompson and Mrs Thompson of Carley Lodge provided 150 poor children who attended the Board Schools with food and clothing over the Christmas and New Year period (1878-79).

At a School Board meeting in May 1879 it was pointed out that distress in the township had led to arrears in the school pence and non-attendance at school. This provoked the chairman W. D. Pratt to say " ... many families were really in so great poverty that the children were compelled to stay at home in an almost naked condition."

In January 1880 Mrs Robert Thompson was thanked by the School Board for her kindness in providing a weekly dinner for seventy children during the previous six weeks; and also for providing 128 dinners for children of the Board Schools on New Years Day.

Although the distress in Southwick was considered not as severe as in neighbouring Sunderland it was necessary to set up a soup kitchen at Low Southwick Mission Room in December 1878. The soup kitchen was financed by the workmen of Southwick industries who made regular weekly contributions. There were initially 150 cases on the books, and half a pound of bread served with one pint of soup to each person three times per week was deemed inadequate by the Southwick Soup Kitchen Committee, which had been set up by workmen of Clark's Engine Works. The Committee made an appeal for donations and organised visits to homes of the unemployed and found that the poverty in Southwick had been underestimated. One of the Committee commented "In several cases we visited it was pitiful to see the poor people anxiously waiting to be relieved by someone, and in Southwick we have not many

gentlemen, but the few we have are doing a great deal of good ..."

Despite the poverty, which would always be a problem in Southwick, there were breathtaking changes throughout the 1870s. Much of Southwick's countryside was lost to house building. Southwick Corn Mill was demolished to make way for Gordon Terrace. Ancient farm cottages on the north side of the Green were flattened and Shakespeare Street was built. New drainage schemes and street improvements were undertaken, a railway (1876); iron shipbuilding replaced wood shipbuilding, with the exception of Pickersgill's which launched the last wood vessel on the Wear – *The Coppername* – in 1880. Clark had brought his large engine building business to Southwick and there was improved postal arrangements to help the township's industries; as well as new telegraph communications with the rest of the country. The character of the people had been tested when Southwick's radical working class fought to maintain a right of way to the Well Field; and

furthermore, the leading citizens had established a School Board and they built new schools. The Local Board continued to look after the township's interests in meetings held to discuss the tramways, a subway under the Wear from Deptford to Southwick, a bridge across the Wear and incorporation. In June 1879 the Local Board sent a letter to the Borough expressing a wish to join with them in their invitation to build a bridge, but strongly stated the Board's opposition to joining Sunderland.

Finally, Southwick appears to have been a relatively healthy place to live in the 1870s. It had a low death rate in comparison with the Borough. Despite deaths in Southwick from typhus, typhoid, small pox, and scarletina, as well as diarrhoea, whooping cough and measles, the township was often free from disease. There is evidence, however, that sanitation problems were festering for future decades especially in the Low Southwick area. A disease free Southwick became a rarity, and the township became infamous for its high infant mortality rate.

After a sewer was damaged during the construction of the railway at Southwick, the Local Board formed a Railway Committee in November 1873 to monitor the work in the interests of the ratepayers. In December 1871 an agreement had been made between the railway company and the Board regarding alterations to Southwick while the railway was being built. However, at a Board meeting in February 1877 James Herring complained that the railway company had carried out work in Southwick without the Board's permission. It appears there was conflict of interests because some of the Board's members were also shareholders of the railway company. James Herring said: "I am afraid to move anything because the railway interest is too strong for me." Chairman Robert Thompson retorted that he was a railway director, but not when he was at Local Board meetings. Mr Herring finally moved that a footpath in Stoney Lane which had been a public right of way for 35 years, and which had been blocked up by the railway company, should be brought to the company's attention. However, the motion was not seconded. "That is just what I said!" declared Mr Herring.

# The 1870s:
# II. Drunkenness, Violence, and Some Strange Goings On!

Southwick could be a violent place in the 1870s when strong and cheap ale, whisky and gin was easily available in the ever increasing number of pubs. Drunken brawls were common, and stand up fights between women, and attacks by men on women often occurred. Many Irish immigrants lived and worked in Southwick. They liked their drink and fought between themselves, with the villagers and with the Police. The Irish were not to blame for all of the trouble of course, and the Police often used physical force to eject drunks who refused to quit beer houses at closing time. There were frequent arrests for drunk and disorderly, drunk and fighting and drunk and riotous. Many Suddickers did not go peacefully and drunkenness was a major problem in Southwick in the 1870s.

## The Reluctant Fighter

On a Friday afternoon in April 1870 Irishman Owen Burns, who worked in a quarry, confronted Andrew Hastie and challenged him to fight. Hastie had walked away from Burns, and a group of men which had gathered outside of Thomas Burdon's beerhouse at the top of Stoney Lane, but he was followed by Burns. Hastie declined to fight and Burns struck him in the face with his fist. Burns attempted to hit him again but Hastie defended himself and returned a blow which flattened Burns. The Irishman hit his head on the kerb as he fell and was knocked out. He was unconscious for six days but when he recovered he was taken back to Ireland by a friend. Andrew Hastie had been arrested and charged with unlawful wounding but the case was dismissed and he was released from prison.

## A Claes Thief

John Docherty was jailed for two months in August 1872 for stealing the clothes of his landlord. He was apprehended in the Three Horse Shoes where he was found wearing two pairs of the landlord's trousers, one inside of the other!

## The Uninvited Guests

Tea was provided for about 600 people at the annual picnic of Holy Trinity Church Sunday School which was held in the grounds of Hylton Castle in August 1872. However, a large gang of roughs sneaked in, and what was described as a 'greedy rampage' ate the food which was intended for others. Teachers organised games for the scholars, but the roughs took the ball from them and took over the field. Several teachers were assaulted by the roughs when they remonstrated with them.

## The Storekeeper's Wife

William Sidney was a storekeeper at Stokoe and Davison's iron shipbuilding yard. In August 1872 he was dismissed for attacking shipyard manager Fenwick Davison who was the brother of one of the partners of the firm. Davison also dismissed Sidney's wife who cleaned the offices. William Sidney was ejected from the yard but waited for Davison outside. Despite the foreman carpenter - described as a tall, powerful man - escorting Davison from the yard, Sidney attacked him again. The next morning Sidney lay in wait for Davison in the yard but he was discovered. Sidney accused Davison of seducing his wife, but was fined £2 and costs for assaulting and threatening Davison.

## Attack on a Policeman

On a Saturday evening in August 1872 at about 8pm a large crowd gathered at Low Southwick while Joseph Phillips and Joseph Matthews fought with PC Mills. The crowd closed in on the policeman and he drew his 'staff'. Ann Riley and Dorothy Gibson were alleged to have assaulted PC Mills, Gibson having seized his staff. Both women denied the assault and were found not guilty. Phillips and Matthews, however, were each fined £1 and costs for the attack on the policeman.

## Friends Free Rioter

On Sunday afternoon 17th November 1872 Michael McMann and his wife Mary Ann assaulted Jane Dagen in Cross Street, Low Southwick. McMann was very drunk and he was shouting and swearing. A large crowd gathered and PC Longstaff took him into custody. Robert Bell, McMann's brother-in-law, followed them into the station and punched the officer. The crowd then rushed in and Frank Kelly released McMann. PC Longstaff explained in court that there had been great difficulty getting witnesses. McMann was fined 10 shillings (50p) and costs for being drunk and riotous. Bell was fined the same amount for assault on PC Longstaff.

Michael McMann was fined again for being drunk in Cross Street on a Saturday night in April 1873. And in July of that year, when his wife was fighting with Elizabeth Fenwick surrounded by a crowd, he was alleged to have kicked her in the head and side while Mrs McMann was on top of her. He denied the charge and the case was dismissed.

## Drunk in Court

The police at Southwick had hard times at weekends but the week ending 16th and 17th November 1872 was particularly busy. Walter Welch was fined 10 shillings and costs for being drunk and riotous. He was shouting that he cared for neither Queen, police or anyone. And William Clark's case of being drunk and riotous had to be adjourned when he appeared in court drunk!

## The Contender

A 30 year old Irish pitman called John Murray of King Street, Low Southwick gave Peter King, an old man, a severe beating in a fight in Pottery Lane. People in the neighbourhood gathered to talk about it and Murray approached them and said, "I'll fight any ten stone man in Southwick!" At one stage the old man's life was in danger but he recovered. The old man dropped the case because he said Murray had a wife and children to support. Murray paid the old man compensation for the assault.

## Old Offenders

Many Southwick men and women were convicted for drunken offences during the 1870s, but there were some who became well known to the County Magistrates. Andrew Oyston was fined the usual fee of 10 shillings and costs for being drunk and disorderly in Mr Dunn's public house. He had caused an uproar after being refused a drink on a Saturday night in November 1873. It was Oyston's 19th appearance before the Bench for drunkenness.

James Wardle had a long history of drunken offences which dated back to 1859. When he appeared before the court on Monday April 16th 1877 it was his 36th appearance. He was fined 10 shillings and costs for being drunk and disorderly at Low Southwick.

Bridget Dooley couldn't appear in court when she was summoned for being drunk and incapable at Southwick on 21st May 1875. She said that she did not have any clothes to wear. Catherine Dooley often caused great disturbances in the streets at Cornhill. In October 1878, when she appeared for the 18th time, she was described as a disgraceful character and was fined £1 and costs.

## An Unfaithful Wife

Patrick Moran was arrested for being drunk and fighting in Clockwell Street on 30th November 1873. However, he was discharged when it was revealed that the man he was fighting with had been caught with his wife. She had since left him with three children to look after.

## A Suspicious Case

George Preston of Cornhill appeared in court in December

1873 accused of assaulting his daughter. Neighbours had contacted the police after beatings by both parents had gone on for about three months. Three neighbours gave evidence that they frequently heard cries and screams coming from the house. They also said that the girl was half starved. On one occasion screams were heard and a neighbour looked through the Preston's window to witness the mother pulling the girl's hair and kicking her. Later in the evening another neighbour heard "a belt going". She looked through the window and saw both the father and mother hitting the girl. The beatings became more intense and Mrs Hone, who lived next door, heard screaming and the sound of blows at about 10.30 pm. Crying continued for about ten minutes and then stopped. The next day the neighbour saw the girl who was badly bruised. She said she had been thrashed by her father and mother and stopped crying after they had put their hands over her mouth. It was then that Mrs Hone contacted the police who visited the house to find Mrs Preston drunk. In the evening both parents were charged with ill using the child and summonses were served. When the police left the Prestons packed up their goods and left home. Both were 'tin-panned' out of the area by neighbours who had gathered. George Preston was apprehended in a drunken state under a haystack in Fulwell Cemetery. When he was searched the police found an insurance policy on him which would pay £8 to the parents if the child died before she was 10 years old. The girl would be ten in two months time! The recent case of Mary Ann Cotton, who had murdered members of her family for to claim the insurance will have been fresh in people's minds. George Preston would not say anything in court and he was sentenced to six months imprisonment. Mrs Preston was still at large. Mrs Hone looked after the girl and the neighbours were highly commended by the Bench.

### 'Blossom'

Late on a Saturday night in April 1874 William Gilley punched and bit PCs Nicholson and Thompson who were arresting him for being drunk and disorderly. Gilley said he could remember nothing of the incident. He was fined 5 shillings (25p) and costs or 21 days in Durham jail; and 20 shillings plus costs or 21 days for the assault. Gilley's cousin had joined in the fracas and he was similarly fined. A large crowd had gathered on The Green to watch the Gilleys fighting with the two policemen. Joseph Henderson was inciting the Gilleys to hit the officers and to resist the arrest. He called upon the crowd to "stone the _____s." The police knew Henderson by the name of 'Blossom', so named because of his "healthful and fully developed physical appearance." Blossom was fined 20 shillings or 21 days in jail.

### A Strange Experience

Ralph Gilley was found asleep in a chair in a pub where six women were drinking in April 1874. When he was aroused by a policeman he was so drunk he could not walk. In court he said. "It was a strange thing - I had not had a drop of beer in the house."

### An Aggravating Wife

John Howard, a blacksmith at Clark's Engine Works was jailed for two months with hard labour for beating up his wife in June 1874. The couple had been married for eight years and had three children, the eldest of which was 5

years old. Mrs Howard said that he regularly beat her and the last occasion was because she had pawned some furniture without her husband's knowledge. She claimed that he did not give her enough money. After the beating she went to stay with her father. Howard visited his wife at her father's house and promised not to hit her again if she returned home with him. Mrs Howard agreed but as soon as they arrived Howard bolted the door and threatened her with the poker. Sarah Howard fell to her knees and begged him to spare her life. "Lie down on the bed and die easy," he demanded. He then hit her with the poker. The Bench remarked that if he had been charged with aggravated assault the sentence would have been longer. Howard replied "It was an aggravated assault I can assure you." The comment was followed by laughter in the courtroom.

### A Family Row

Late on Saturday night on 26th September 1874 a neighbourhood in Southwick was in uproar when male and female members of the McLeod family fought with each other in the house. By the time PC Thompson arrived the mother Catherine had a black eye, her daughter was unconscious on the floor with a cut eye, and the son, John, was attacking the father. John McLeod was drunk and he turned on the officer. PC Thompson arrested McLeod but while he was taking him into custody the officer was surrounded by a large crowd which included members of the McLeod family. Kate McLeod and Ann Roper got hold of the constable's arms and hit him. The officer was also struck with a brick which was thrown from the crowd, and John McLeod was freed by the mob. The family were dealt with in

court. The mother, Catherine McLeod, was also fined for being drunk the day after the trouble. She was in trouble again in July 1875 when she was involved in an argument with Margaret Donnelly at the latter's front door. McLeod spat in Donnelly's face several times and was fined 5 shillings and costs for the offence. When Margaret Donnelly made her way home after the court hearing she was approached by McLeod's daughter who was described as a "stylishly dressed young lady". The daughter hit Donnelly across the face. She returned to report the assault to the court and McLeod's daughter was brought before the Bench and fined 15 shillings (75p) and costs or 14 days in jail.

### Hands in the Till

On an afternoon in June 1875 16 year old David Wood and 17 year old Thomas Houston went into the Victoria Inn at Low Southwick and ordered two glasses of beer. After serving them the barmaid went into another room and left the boys alone. She heard the noise of money and returned to the bar. The lads had gone and the empty till was lying on the floor. Wood and Houston were apprehended by the police and were each jailed for three months for taking £1 from the till.

### The Good Templar

In September 1875 William Hayton hit Joseph Graham, a cripple, with a knuckle duster because he had reformed by stopping drinking and joined The Good Templars. Hayton was warned by the Bench not to interfere with Graham again.

### Disturbing a Boozing Session

Sarah Lathan went to a public house to find her husband on July 23rd 1876. When she entered the pub she found him asleep. She went to wake him but Joseph Stewart who was drinking there, exchanged angry words with her. Stewart punched and kicked the woman and made her bleed profusely. The noise woke the husband who hit Stewart over the head with a chair. Stewart was fined 2s 6d (121/2p) and costs.

## The Accused Policeman

PC Nicholson appeared in court accused of being drunk and urinating on John Brown while he stood at the bus stand at Southwick with three friends on July 30th 1876.

Brown said that he went to the police station to complain and on the way he saw PC Nicholson lying on The Green drunk with three other men. The constable had served for 16 years in the police force and he was of previous good character and service. It was said in his defence that a group of men at Southwick had a grudge against him because he had reason to charge them. The case against PC Nicholson was dismissed. At the same hearing in August 1876 Joseph Stewart and Thomas Brown were charged with assaulting PC Nicholson at about midnight on Saturday 12th August at Southwick. A cross summons was brought by Stewart and Brown who claimed that PC Nicholson was sitting on a window sill and he was drunk. Brown said to him "You are drunk you b_____ get up. Everybody is looking at you there." PC Nicholson was said to have got up and hit Brown before he staggered back to the window sill. Several witnesses verified the story. PC Nicholson was found not guilty but Stewart was fined 10 shillings (50p) and Brown 5 shillings (25p) for the assault on the officer.

## Rival Cartmen

Mathew Garratt was a powerfully built man who hawked fish in the streets of Southwick. On 23rd February 1877 he was drinking in the Portsmouth Arms at Low Southwick. Wilkinson, the coal hawker, was drinking there too. As the evening wore on the drink began to loosen their tongues and both men bragged on their ability as salesmen. The competition and arguments became heated and finally Garratt challenged Wilkinson, who was a much smaller man, to fight him for £20. At this point Joseph Thompson who was also drinking in the pub pushed Garratt into a seat. Garratt got up but Thompson struck him in the face with his fist and Garratt went down. Thompson said "I've owed you that for a long time." Thompson was fined 20 shillings and costs for the assault.

## The Unpopular Bailiff

On 2nd June 1877 at about 12 noon Robert Smart, a bailiff, visited the home of the Thompson family in Carley Street to issue a distress warrant. He entered the house and was about to read the warrant when Mrs Thompson shouted - "Put the b_____ out!" She got hold of Smart's whiskers, Mr Thompson grabbed him by the throat and assisted by their daughters, Sarah and Margaret, the family bundled him out of the door. The son, Joseph, shouted - "Let me at the _____ !" Joseph and his two willing sisters grabbed hold of Smart's coat and whiskers and threw him into the street. Joseph Thompson continued the attack with a knuckle duster. He knocked out the bailiff, cutting his lip wide open in the process. When the bailiff regained consciousness he came back to the house with a

policeman, and the warrant, which ordered a payment of 15 shillings and 3d, was read to the Thompson's. The family paid Smart the money but a large crowd had gathered and they pelted the bailiff with stones while the Thompson's swore and threatened him as he was walking away.

## The Tramp's Trap

A tramp dressed in old ragged clothes was served a pint of beer at the West Country Arms at Low Southwick. It was 8.30 on a Sunday morning in June 1877. The pub was full and overflowed into the street where there was a large crowd. One man was so drunk that he fell into the street. Michael Oliver, the landlord, was charged with opening his licensed premises during prohibited hours and he was fined 10 shillings and costs. The tramp had been PC Mills in disguise. The landlord was placed on the 'Black List' of the Brewster Sessions which issued licenses to sell alcohol in the Sunderland Division. Although Michael Oliver's license was renewed in August 1877, he was called up to appear at the sessions where he was severely admonished.

## Thoughtful Landlord

Edward Dunn of the Mill Inn on The Green sold Inspector Harrison a pint of whisky for two shillings (10p) in October 1877 which was found to be thirty per cent under proof. He explained in court that he was not guilty because he had "an eye for humanity and diluted the whisky with water." Robert Graham, who kept the Smiths Arms next door was also fined 10 shillings and costs for watering down the whisky.

## "I'll Break Your Neck!"

In December 1877 William Nelson said he saw PC Warren strike a man over the fingers with a stick, and it looked to him that the officer "was trying to cause mischief instead of peace." Nelson remonstrated with the constable, whereupon the officer was alleged to have threatened to break Nelson's neck. Nelson threw off his coat and challenged the officer to fight. The Bench asked Nelson if he threw off his coat. "Yes Sir," replied Nelson. "When I was told he would break my neck. It's a very hard case if a man has to stand and have his neck broken!" Nelson was fined 2s-6d (12½p) and costs for being drunk and disorderly.

## Legless!

In April 1878 James Meeghan was found "incapably drunk" in Fulwell Lane. He was taken to Southwick in a cart. When he appeared in court he was ordered to pay for the ride as well as the normal fine and costs.

## Mistaken Identity

William Gibbons, who was described as a "powerful looking man" quarrelled with his wife in October 1877. Gibbons became enraged and Mrs Gibbons ran into a neighbours backyard to escape his wrath. Josephine Waggeland and her mother were in the yard when the drunken Gibbons appeared in pursuit of his wife. He mistook the young woman, Josephine, for his wife and thumped her in the face so hard that he knocked out several of her teeth. He pulled the hair out of her head and hit her about the body. Gibbons disappeared from Southwick for several days after the assault, but he was arrested on his return. He pleaded guilty to aggravated assault and was sent to Durham jail for two months with hard labour.

## Conclusion

Clergy, leading businessmen and residents of Southwick were concerned over the madness and resulting poverty caused by alcohol abuse by some of the poorly educated portion of the community. Something had to be done about the large number of Southwick men and women who used the beer and spirit houses to escape from their harsh lives. On at least one occasion during the 1870s the Police News section of the *Sunderland Times* recorded a list of people dealt with by the County Magistrates under the heading – "Southwick Drunkards".

However, in a community like Southwick where drink was a big problem the temperance movement was strongly represented. Suddickers were encouraged to 'Sign the Pledge'. Teetotal Methodists were a force in Southwick. There was the alcohol free Southwick Workmen's Institute, the Good Templars and temperance lectures.

At the Brewster Sessions at Sunderland for the County Division in August 1877, the Rev C.S. Collingwood presented three petitions on behalf of the people of Southwick to protest against the increase of premises for selling alcohol at the rapidly expanding Carley Place and Cornhill. Almost all of the manufacturing premises in the township had signed one of the petitions. Robert Thompson and Anthony Scott had added their names. They were deeply interested in the 'serious evils' to which they all were exposed by the large number of licensed houses in Southwick. Furthermore, it was stated that people living in the immediate neighbourhood of Carley Place dreaded the prospect of extending the current beer off licence to a combined beer off and beer on licensed premises. Ninety residents of Carley Place had signed a memorial because they did not wish their neighbourhood to have the drink related problems like Cornhill was experiencing.

Mr Collingwood presented a third memorial to the Brewster Sessions in August 1877 on behalf of Southwick School Board. The Board saw themselves as the Guardians of Southwick children, and they were acutely aware of the suffering caused by "the extensive indulgence in intoxicating drinks amongst the inhabitants." The memorial read:

"Your memorialists are deeply impressed with the evils resulting from the already abounding facilities for the sale of intoxicating liquors in this district, and especially as those evils effect the children of parents who indulge in drink. Your memorialists therefore have most earnestly to request your worships to grant no new licenses for the township of Southwick, and that you will earnestly enforce all restrictions upon the holders of existing licenses, and as far as possible reduce their number."

The decision of this court at the annual Brewster Sessions in August 1877 refused all applications to sell alcohol on the premises. Southwick School Board were again successful in their petition signed by three hundred people in August 1878 against the application of a full licence at the Albion Hotel in Southwick Lane which was only allowed to sell beer. The School Board was determined to prevent the issue of new licences in the township. Indeed, they were ambitious to do all in their power to reduce the number of public houses in Southwick to curb the 'drink traffic' owing to the "constant and painful evidence of the mischief which drink is doing in the district."

# Characters and Personalities

## Sir William Mills the inventor

William Mills was born in Southwick in 1856. According to the 1861 census he was living in Wear Street, Southwick with his father David (39) who is described as a 'ship joiner', his mother Sarah Ann (39), and his two brothers and two sisters.

Corder records that David Mills had an interest in the Mills shipbuilding firm but it was run by his brothers George and John.

By 1871 the family had moved to 22 Camden Street. David Mills is recorded as a 'joiner'. Fourteen-year-old William left school and served a seven year apprenticeship with George Clark's. Afterwards he spent several years at sea and in 1884 obtained a first class certificate as a marine engineer. This explains his omission from the 1881 census return where his father David (59) is described as a 'retired shipowner', residing in Camden Street. David Mills the Southwick shipbuilder is buried in the family tomb in Southwick cemetery.

No doubt William Mills' experiences at sea stirred a curiosity for the need of a system to release ship's lifeboats when they were lowered into the water. Motivated by the great loss of life caused by an inadequate system in use at that time, William Mills invented a simple, safe and efficient method for instantaneously engaging and disengaging the hooks on ship's lifeboats on entering the water. When the invention was exhibited in 1886 at the Liverpool Shipowners' Exhibition he was awarded the Gold Medal of the Mercantile Marine Service Association, and the Exhibition Gold Medal. The Board of Trade approved the system and it came into world-wide use in both naval and merchant ships.

William Mills opened the UK's first aluminium foundry in 1885 at Bonnersfield, Monkwearmouth, and later opened another branch in Birmingham. He produced lightweight aluminium castings for the car and aircraft industries.

He was an amateur golfer and improved the design of the aluminium golf club. Mills tackled the problem of wooden drivers which were handmade and difficult for golfers to replace after acquiring a 'feel' for a favourite club. He had a wealth of manufacturing knowledge and his design the 'Mills Standard' driver was marketed in 1895 or 1896, and was produced in large numbers. It enabled golfers to replace worn or broken drivers with an identical one. He "... perfected a product in an area where none had succeeded before, earning himself recognition in history as the godfather of the metal wood" – Georgiady 1993.

William Mills was also the inventor of a telescopic walking stick seat, but his most important invention earned him a knighthood. In 1915 he opened his Mills Munition factory in Birmingham to produce the Mills Bomb, more commonly known as the hand grenade. Seventy-five million were made for the Allies which were extensively and successfully used during the First World War.

Sir William Mills died in 1932 at Western-super-Mare. He was married for about forty years. His wife had died in 1930. He left £37,839 - 11s - 9d net, which seems a relatively small amount when considering the inventions he manufactured in his own factories, and the fact that he had no children. It is perhaps interesting to point out that when he received £27,750 from the government for the Mills Bomb invention he failed in his efforts to avoid paying income tax on the sum. He claimed that he had lost money by the grenade.

*The Mills family tomb in Southwick Cemetery*

Sources
1. Oxford Dictionary of National Biography 1931-40
2. Golfiana Volume 5 Number 2 (1993) - The Godfather of the Metal Wood by Peter Georgiady
3. The Corder Manuscripts
4. Various Local Newspapers
5. Census Returns 1861, 1871, 1881.

St Hilda's R.C. School football team 1956-57. Back row left to right: Billy Kibble, Peter Conlon, Mickey McMann, Jimmy Montgomery, Joe Lane, George Askew. Front row: Albert Middlemiss, John Bartley, Tony Smith, Jas Clark, Terry McBay.

PC Jim Weatherill with his son Stephen in about 1958. Southwick man Jim was on the the beat at Southwick from 1964-67.

Les Cooper returned to the bridge in 1985 where his brother Robert (right) was photographed sixty-five years previously. The bridge was removed about three or four years

Local men and children (some barefoot) pose on the railway bridge which led from Camden Street (left) to Clockwell Street (right) in 1920. Second boy from the left is Robert Cooper. He lost his life when he was knocked down by a hit and run driver in Hendon Road in c. 1992. He was eighty-two.

Holy Trinity Church Lads Brigade at the front of the Rectory in 1932/ 33.

Southwick boxer Paddy Lynch in about 1911. Paddy fought locally for a 'few bob' a fight.

## Jack Washington

*Above: Jack Washington as opening bat for Sunderland at Ashbrooke in about 1952.*

When Jack Washington of John Street was married in June 1943 he was described as "an outstanding sportsman". He attended High Southwick School and played cricket and football for Sunderland Boys. He progressed in the local leagues and played cricket for Sunderland First Team for about 30 years. Jack was a good batsman and an exceptional fielder. He was chosen to play for Durham County as 12th man (because of his fielding ability) against the West Indies, India, Australia and New Zealand. Jack remembers with nostalgia when big crowds attended top local games of cricket and football.

On the football scene he played in goal for Bishop Auckland with former Liverpool manager Bob Paisley. Jack played in three Amateur Cup Finals with 'Bishops' – losing two and winning one. In the 1950 Cup Final he played in front of 83,000 at Wembley. Jack enjoyed his football and couldn't understand how people got upset about it. Contemporary newspaper reports on games describe him as a – "a brilliant amateur goalkeeper who smiled his way through 20 years of top class amateur football." And with a height disadvantage of 5 ft 6 $1/4$ ins – "his remarkable agility made up for his lack of inches."

Eighty-two-year-old Jack recalls with pride that at his peak he could run 100 yards in 10 seconds. However, he saw himself as a local footballer who didn't quite have that little bit extra to make it professionally. But, nonetheless he got immense satisfaction out of pleasing the spectators.

Jack served in the war from 1939-45 and afterwards became a PE teacher in Sunderland Schools.

*Jack with a photograph of himself during the 1950 Amateur Cup Final at Wembley.*

Southwick man Gordon Howe, In October 1996, holding the citation he received from FIFA for his services to football. Gordon started the Sunderland Sunday League in 1958, the Sunderland Over 40s league in 1980, and the Sunderland Over 35s in 1983. The idea for the Over 40s League was unique and Gordon was subjected to some ridicule. "They said that I was crackers and the players would need oxygen masks!" said 66-year-old Gordon. However, undaunted and despite the comments and people's stereotypes regarding footballers, Gordon turned his idea into a reality. The over 40s League has been a remarkable success and the first of its kind in the world.

Sixteen years on and the League is still growing while many young men's leagues in the area are in decline.

A new career awaits footballers who reach the age of 40. Many local players are thankful to Gordon Howe for his 'brainchild'.

In September 1996 79-year-old Jossy Wilson holds the Distinguished Service Award he received in 1984 from Durham C.I.U. in recognition for forty years service with the working men's club movement. Jossy retired in 1992.

Southwick Social Club Committee (early 1960s) Left to right: Arthur Watson, Gowan Scott, Billy Foster, Albert Watson (he became Mayor in 1965), Billy Wakinshaw, Billy Lloyd, Charlie Burnett, Joe McCormick. Front row: Tommy Goldsmith, Jossy Wilson, John Carter, Jim Davis.

### Charlotte Chambers

Charlotte Chambers (c.1893 - 1965) was reputed to have been the first woman chimney sweep in Southwick (and perhaps the only one). She took over her husband Terry's round when he was called up in 1939. The round was mainly on the north side of the river and a sweep's licence cost 7s 6d (37$\frac{1}{2}$p) per year. Charlotte charged 1s 6d (7$\frac{1}{2}$p) per chimney but by the time she retired from the job in 1957-58 she was charging 2s 6d (12$\frac{1}{2}$p). She swept miners' chimney's and some paid her in coal which she often gave to hard up families. The Chambers lived at 76, Maplewood Avenue which was next to the cut that led to the football field and Summerbell Allotments. Charlotte took over her husband's allotments during the war. She also cultivated her own garden and a wartime allotment in North Hylton Road, a site later occupied by Plessey, and more recently by factory units. Charlotte displayed her produce for sale at the side of the house. She also sold milk for a local farmer and soot to gardeners for fertiliser. Charlotte Chambers was a busy character indeed.

St Columba's Scouts, Cubs, Guides, Brownies and Leaders. Low Sunday 1956.

In the Tram Car Inn, 1954. Left to right PC Maurice Fletcher, manager of the Tram Car, PC Alf Davison. Alf Davison served on the beat at Southwick and he lived in Old Mill Road. He recalls that he was kept busy in Southwick, but despite having to deal with rough lads and men, he had no problems living in the community.

## Eddie Rowley (1921 - c. 1981)

Eddie Rowley is pictured sitting outside of his pigeon cree with his dog 'Blackie'. He loved animals from an early age and on one occasion he brought a nanny goat home with him. Eddie took the goat to school one day but Mr Carrick, the headmaster at St Columba's, wouldn't let the pet into school. So Eddie played 'the doll' (truant) with the goat. Eddie didn't like school and avoided going as much as possible. His education obviously suffered and in later years when he was working away from home his mother had difficulty reading his letters: "Dear Maw, send me two shits (shirts) and a pair of boats (boots)."

On another occasion when he was a lad his mother gave him a dog – a thoroughbred she said it was. But young Eddie wasn't impressed: "Ere Maw, ah thowt yay sez 'ee was a thoroughbred?" He complained the next morning. A frustrated Eddie was sitting on the floor beside a puzzled looking dog, and numerous crusts of bread which he had been trying to feed to it!

When he left school Eddie started work at the pit but the management sent for his dad when they found out about his severely disabled left arm. Eddie had disguised it well enough and he was a good worker, but the management were concerned that he could have an accident. Afterwards he worked in the shipyards as a rivet heater. Eddie was forced to do everything with his 'good arm' and he built up a considerable amount of strength with it.

Over the years Eddie usually owned a dog. He called one of them "Help". The bairns would call him by name – "Help, Help", and grown ups would run from all directions to see what was wrong. Eddie was a jolly, humorous character who was well known in Southwick pubs. He loved to tell jokes and his hysterical loud laughter was infectious. After a few pints his favourite song was 'Billy Boy'. If he got into trouble he could use his disabled arm as a weapon. He couldn't feel anything but the victim could!

Every New Year's Eve the family held a party at Mrs Rowley's in Shakespeare Street. All of the relations were invited and the children too. The inevitable fight would take place between Eddie and his brother Harry. There are memories of the women of the family opening the windows and frantically passing the children into the garden until things were sorted out. The party would continue when brothers Harry and Eddie were best of mates again.

Another of Eddie's activities was collecting snails, cooking and flogging (selling) them. He was warned off by a farmer at Whitburn on one occasion for almost demolishing an old stone wall to get at the snails.

Many Southwick people have a tale to tell about Eddie Rowley. There's the one about the time he built sections of a pigeon cree in the scullery of his mother's home. When he tried to get it out of the back door it was two inches too big and he had to dismantle it again.

There's another about the time he went to the doctor complaining of piles. The doctor prescribed some medication. After the second dose he complained to his mother that it tasted horrible – "They're trying to poison me!" he exclaimed.
"It's a suppository," said Mrs Rowley, "You daft bugger, you put it in the other end!"

Eddie suffered a heart attack but recovered a little. It was his last wish that when he died the hearse should pass by the Southwick pubs where he had so many good times (this was arranged). In hospital he said to his brother Harry: "If anything happens to me, when the funeral passes The Sun Inn stop the hearse and pop in for a quick pint; and leave me outside like you've always done. You greedy b_____." Eddie then burst into loud laughter. Shortly afterwards he had a relapse and died. "Yes, he joked to the end," recalls his sister Elsie.

After Eddie's funeral service hundreds of pigeons were released to greet his coffin on the way out of St Columba's Church.

Above: Both sides of Lilian Reid's silver medal which she received from Sunderland Education Authority for her remarkable 100% attendance record.

Lilian Reid (later Fletcher) attended High Southwick School from 1919 to 1928 without losing one day through absence. Lilian is pictured front row second from left with the school netball team.

High Southwick Junior School football team 1955-56. League Champions and Watson Cup winners. Back row left to right: Mr Kelsall, Mr Moore, Mr Finney. Middle row: T. Holden, A. Donaldson, P. Barr, D. Craggs, W. McGarley, D. Nelson, W. Donkin, D. Duncan, M. Fenwick. Front row: J. King, R. Linstead, I. Pearn, R. Graham, R. Brown, B. Lawson, C. Henderson.

In the late 1970s a 'wedding' took place as part of the Easter holiday entertainment in the Smiths Arms. Tommy Harvey senior 'married' the 'bride' Blonde Nellie pictured centre. Tommy Keegan (right) was 'the best man' and congratulates Mr Harvey on his good fortune.

These three little characters create a heart warming scene in Back Stoney Lane in 1951. Left to right sisters and brother Pat, Margaret and Barry Herkes.

Mrs Price at the back door of the Banks of the Wear pub. She was in the pub for forty-two years from 1906 until she died in 1948 aged sixty-eight.

West Southwick Boys School. Class of c. 1946, plus dog.

A rare undated photograph of the Banks of the Wear Hotel in King Street, Low Southwick. The building was demolished and rebuilt in 1909.

High Southwick School cricket team in 1954.

## Doctor Dickey

Dr Thomas Dickey (1895-1970) (above) was a well known GP in Southwick. He lived in Southwick House with his wife Jenny and their children. Jenny was a trained midwife although she became a housewife after she married, and helped her husband to run the practice. They had three children William and Mary, pictured above, and then later Peter. Sadly William died of leukaemia aged $4\frac{1}{2}$. Dr Dickey was an Irishman and he could be very blunt when the need arose, recalls his daughter Mary. But he was very much part of the community as a family doctor. The Dickey family are photographed above in about 1950/51 in the grounds of Southwick House. Behind the high walls in the background is King's Road.

# Lewis Carroll, A Walrus, A Carpenter and Holy Trinity Church Rectory, Southwick

## By Rev Robert Dixon – Rector of Holy Trinity Church

The connection between Lewis Carroll and the Rectory, Holy Trinity Church, Southwick, is well recorded both in the author's own voluminous letters and recorded by the various biographers this century. When Mary Dodgson married the Rector, the Reverend Charles Edward Stuart Collingwood, the correspondence and visits by Lewis Carroll, her brother, began a link which was to bear literary fruit, and perhaps, give Southwick a share in the creation of part of the writings of Alice and her adventures. (Lewis Carroll being the pseudonym of the Reverend Charles Dodgson.) Carroll's visits to the North East can also be associated with two cousins who lived in Whitburn, close to Seaburn, Sunderland.

Throughout the books about Alice there are poems, one of which is a memorable story of a chance meeting of two very singular individuals on the beach and the conversation that ensued. Out of that exchange came a phrase which has found a life of its own away from the poem, and is now an accepted term to describe a conversation of little consequence but of no small intensity.

Whilst the following sequence of events are founded on both documented and hearsay records, I have added, perhaps rather fancifully my own thoughts on how the story of the Walrus and the Carpenter originated. On one of Lewis Carroll's visits to the Rectory, he went for a customary walk along Seaburn Beach towards Roker, and by chance met a ship's carpenter – they sat down on the beach and talked:

"Of shoes – and ships – and sealing wax –
Of cabbages – and kings –"

When Carroll returned to the Rectory at Southwick, on entering the hall he would have been greeted by a large stuffed walrus. It was often the custom, in Victorian parish life, that when a church-goer returned from some great journey or endeavour in the distant climes of the British Empire, they would bring back some gift or token of their travels. To this day there are many churchyards, or clergy gardens that have exotic plants or trees, or perhaps statuary, given by some traveller of the last century. The walrus at the Southwick Rectory obviously marked some journey that caused Lewis Carroll to consider it worthy of being immortalised in a poem. As to the ship's carpenter, the square hat shown in Tenniel's evocative drawings are known to have been worn by those craftsmen of the Sunderland shipyards massed along the banks of the River Wear.

Perhaps after a good lunch, an eventful walk with its chance meeting on Seaburn Beach, the sight of that guardian walrus on his return to Southwick Rectory; and as Carroll rested beneath one of the many trees in the Rectory garden the Muse of poetic inspiration gave new life to that moment.

For the rest of his life Lewis Carroll was a frequent visitor to the Rectory at Southwick. He was known to have organised, devised and often written 'little entertainments' for the Rector and his wife, Mary, with their own family and many of the children of their household staff and of the Parish. The last recorded letter that Carroll sent to the Rectory provided also to be the penultimate of all his letters. The Rector, Mr Collingwood, had died and Carroll wrote that because of his own infirmity he would not be able to attend the funeral at Holy Trinity Church, but he enclosed £50 to help with the funeral expenses.

At the beginning of this passage it has been indicated that the link between Lewis Carroll and the Rectory at Holy Trinity Church, Southwick, is well documented. So with a little of our own literary imagination is it not possible that the creator of Alice gave life to the walrus and the carpenter as I have suggested?

*The Walrus and the Carpenter*
*Walked on a mile or so,*
*And then they rested on a rock*
*Conveniently low:*
*And all the little Oysters stood*
*And waited in a row.*

*'The time has come', the Walrus said,*
*'To talk of many things:*
*Of shoes – and ships – and sealing wax –*
*Of cabbages – and kings –*
*And why the sea is boiling hot –*
*And whether pigs have wings.'*

Extracts of *Through The Looking Glass* by Lewis Carroll.

*Rev C. S. Collingwood.     Mrs Mary Collingwood.*

*Holy Trinity Rectory in 1996.*

*Lewis Carroll who often visited his sister at Southwick Rectory (photograph from the Carroll family collection.)*

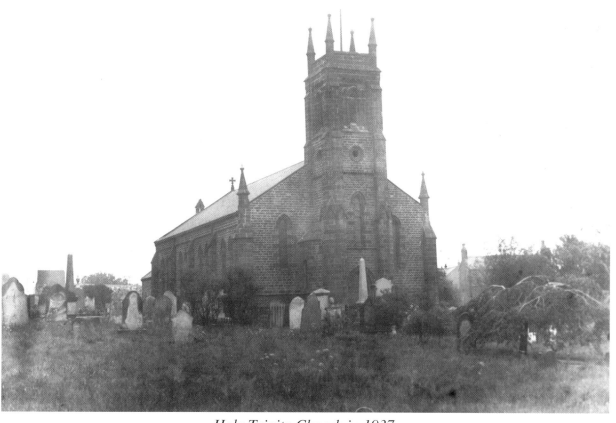

*Holy Trinity Church in 1937.*

# 1930s Scrapbook

March 15th, 1930 - Southwick G.P. and surgeon Dr John Joseph Carruthers of Park House, The Green collapsed and died in the grandstand at Roker Park while he was watching Sunderland play football. Dr Carruthers was the Medical Officer of Health for Southwick's Council and he left an estate valued at £6,391 (See Southwick-on-Wear Vol.3 P. 12).

May 24th, 1930 - A new children's playground was opened at Carley by Wearmouth Miners' Welfare. At the beginning of June there was a fatality when seven year old Thomas Southern Bailey of 32 Wellington Street fell 15 feet from the top of the 'Slidey' onto his head.

*The slide where the fatality occurred.*

July 16th, 1930 - The property Market was described as slow. 30, Florence Crescent was sold for £255, and a cottage at Hawthorne Street, Carley Place was sold for £115.

During the summer of 1930 a plague of rabbits, more than there had ever been seen before, infested the allotment gardens at Marley Pots and ate the vegetables. One gardener complained that the rabbits would come out in front of him to eat his produce without even a "by your leave!" But when it was arranged for lads to lie in wait for them with air guns to reduce the numbers they would not come out, just as if they knew.

August 9th, 1930 - PC Hutchinson was on duty on The Terrace (now Southwick Road) when he apprehended William H. of Suddick Street on suspicion of street betting. When William H was searched three betting slips were found hidden in his false leg! The case was dismissed and he was released with a warning.

September 9th, 1930 - A gang of boys broke into West Southwick school. They were discovered by the caretaker and after a chase escaped over a wall. It was found that they had raided the larder and cooked a meal for themselves on the gas range but left the washing up!

September 16th, 1930 - the foundation stone of Southwick Branch Library was laid by Alderman J.S. Nicholson. A dedicatory prayer was said by Rev E.W. Bolland of Southwick Parish Church. Alderman Harry Brown, a former headmaster of High Southwick Schools, thanked the corporation on behalf of the people of Southwick and said, "Southwick is the largest ward in the Borough and a ward of working men, but we have a soul above money making... As an old teacher I would like to say how much we appreciate this opportunity of having a library in our midst."

February 18th, 1931 - An unusual auction took place at Sir John Priestman's shipyard. A cargo steamer of 4,350 tons deadweight was on the berth and ready to be launched. However, a Norwegian company which ordered the vessel cancelled the contract and vessel number 299 was left on Priestman's hands. Councillor Potts began the bidding with an offer of £10,000. Mr Pinkney the auctioneer said, "It is very kind of you, but which part of the ship do you want to buy?" Which was followed by loud laughter among those present. Following a bid of £20,000 the steamer was withdrawn from auction.

*Southwick Branch Library was opened on September 16th 1931 by the Mayor Ald E.H. Brown. A large crowd witnessed the opening.*

March 25th, 1931 - There was anti - Conservative feeling at a well attended meeting in the Savoy Picture Hall. 'Rowdies' did their best to disrupt the proceedings by booing and stamping when the speakers made their appearance on stage. Sir John Priestman presided and made an appeal for fair play.- "I am a Southwick man myself, and I appeal to you to give the speakers a sportsman-like hearing, even if you do not agree with them." There was quiet for a short time but the speakers had a hard time and were continually interrupted throughout the afternoon.

April 4th, 1931 - On this day a wedding took place at St Columba's Church which astonished a taxi driver. He picked up the bride at Chilton Street, the daughter of Mr and Mrs C.L. Howarth. The Sunderland Echo reported - "... Then he sat back to wait until the ceremony was over. 'There are two more to come' said the best man. 'Two more what?' asked the taxi driver. 'Two more brides!' Martha (28), Isabella (23) and Elizabeth (20) were being married to bridegrooms at the same ceremony. It was the first triple wedding at St Columba's and a large crowd gathered outside of the church to see the brides.

April 23rd, 1931 - Joseph Wailes of 30 Carley Road died in the Municipal Hospital. He was a freeman of the Borough which had been presented to him and others who had volunteered to fight in the Boer War. Joseph Wailes also served during the First World War and he was badly gassed. He suffered for many years from the effects which finally caused his death at the age of 51.

June 1st, 1931 - Southwick folklore and legend was rekindled and great interest was aroused by the discovery of an underground tunnel and chamber. Workmen broke into the passages while working on West House which was situated on Church Bank at the extreme west end of Southwick Green (the site is now occupied by Lord Gort Close). For generations there had been talk of a series of secret underground tunnels. The discovered vaulted chamber measured about 10 feet by 6 feet and it was possible to stand in a stooped position. Small stalactites hung from the arched roof and the walls were of rubble and dressed stone similar to that of Hylton Castle. The chamber exit was blocked up by large stones. West House was built in the early part of the 19th century and it was

discovery workmen at the end of Clockwell Street, about 200 yards from West House, found some ancient remains of similar materials and construction as found at the West House site.

November 23rd, 1931 - John H. of Brougham Street, Low Southwick, was fined £20 for keeping a betting house. His wife was fined £5 for assisting in the management. Police had kept a watch on the house and recorded 92 visits in one hour. Many of the 'gamblers' were boys and girls who were involved in a dinner hour rush to the house. Mrs H objected when the police wanted to search the house and she said, "There are plenty more of them (bookmakers) up the street!"

*The secret chamber which was accidentally discovered beneath West House in June 1931.*

occupied by Henry Scott who died in 1854. He was a member of the Scott family who owned the pottery. Henry Scott owned the bottleworks. An inspection of the chamber suggested that it was constructed long before West House. Mr H Batty, the resident at the time of the discovery, thought that Henry Scott may have discovered the old passages and had them reconstructed for use as wine cellars. Shortly before this

**They Had 22 Children!**

Mr and Mrs James Edward Mann of 15 Mary Street were married at Southwick Parish Church on January 17th 1882. They celebrated their golden wedding in 1932. 69 year old Mr Mann and his 68 year old wife had 22 children, eleven of whom were living in Sunderland.

April 9th, 1932 - It was announced that Robert Thompson and Sons Shipyard would close down permanently and the site cleared. The yard had been purchased by the National Shipbuilding Securities Ltd, which was an organisation formed to close and scrap redundant shipyards. The announcement highlighted the fact that the Descobridor and Cort Real were the last vessels built at the yard. They were the world's largest trawlers but were left on the builders hands when the Portuguese owners defaulted in payment. The auction of plant and machinery took place at the yard on June 8th 1932.

November 28th, 1932 - After six months as Headmaster of West Southwick School Mr Kelsall revealed the philosophy of the school which was proving to be successful. A happy atmosphere was encouraged and acknowledged as an important aspect of school life. Mr Kelsall said, "Everything else fails unless the boys are happy and the driving force is inspiration instead of fear. The latter only kills the initiative one aims at attaining for these boys. We encourage a happy atmosphere - to us a laugh is a sign of progress. When Mr Kelsall came to the school he said that between twenty and thirty boys attended school in bare feet. He pointed out that older boys in families were doing without shoes so that their younger brothers and sisters in the infant school could have shoes. With the cooperation of parents the school encouraged the boys to help each other out with clothes and shoes. Six months into the scheme and not a boy was in the unfortunate position of not wearing shoes for school. Boys were not forced to do homework which was seen as a privilege and not a task. Mr Kelsall pointed out that 'teachers were astounded' by the

*West Southwick School Infants playing on the May Pole in 1932/33. Ken Lay is on the left. Third boy from left is Len harper who grew up to become a Southwick councillor and Mayor of Sunderland.*

number of boys who voluntarily ask if they can do homework!"

November 29th, 1932 - On this day Southwick contributed to the political history of the town when a bye election took place in Southwick to fill the vacant seat on the Town Council caused by Peter Inglis becoming an alderman. Mr J Harvey (socialist) defeated W.H.Austin who was the Independent Anti-Socialist Candidate. Southwick became the

first ward in Sunderland to have a complete socialist representation on the Town Council of an alderman and councillors.

An unemployed Southwick man committed suicide by cutting his throat with a razor. He was found on a path leading to Carley Hill quarry. He had been wounded in the Great War and since then he had suffered with his nerves, pains in the head and insomnia. A note was found in his pocket: "Dear _____

*Lads playing on the climbing cage (which became known as the 'monkey climber') at the new playground in Thompson Park – March 1933.*

look after the little ones as you have always done. You have been a good wife to me. Sorry to cause you this trouble."

May 9th, 1933 - The *Echo* writer "From a Window in Bridge Street" commented: "A distinctive feature at Southwick is the number of dogs in the district. I counted no fewer than twenty three dogs one day playing on The Oval. There was very little bickering and it seemed to be an accepted playground where a state of armed neutrality existed. I say armed neutrality because when an apparently strange dog appeared, three or four 'regulars' sent him flying into Southwick Road - and the others looked on and seemed prepared for battle if necessary."

*Children playing on what became known as the 'Lazy Liz' at Thompson Park in March 1933.*

### Best in the Town

During the summer of 1933 the gardens of council house tenants on the Marley Pots estate were reported to have been the best kept in the town. The garden of almost every house had been utilised for fruit and vegetables and laid out in flower beds. The tenants were a credit to Southwick.

January 24th, 1934 - A letter appeared in the *Echo* complaining about "slum people" being moved onto the Marley Pots estate among respectable tenants. The writer went on to point out that a gang of young men regularly played noisy games of football on the Marley Pots estate on Sundays. "...If this state of affairs is to be allowed we are going to feel as if we are living in some degraded place."

In January 1934 27-year-old Mrs Alice Wilson of Back Carley Road died of burns after her clothing caught fire at home. The coroner praised the "meritorious actions"

of Thomas O'Brien, also of Carley Road who put out the flames with a mat. Another neighbour Mrs Patterson was also praised for treating Mrs Wilson's burns.

1935 – Nixon Rowell of Southwick set up a new British weight lifting record with a clean lift and jerk of 209 lb. The previous record was 206 $\frac{1}{2}$ lb.

April 24th, 1935 – Mrs S.S. Worthy is pictured cutting the cake at the 75th birthday celebrations of Clockwell Street Methodist Church. The streamers and banners, which were used for the 50th anniversary in 1910, were used again to decorate the Church Hall in Dean Terrace where the 75th anniversary party took place.

## The Loyal Order of Ancient Shepherds Friendly Society
## Pride of Southwick Lodge
### by Arthur Turnbull

In the late nineteenth century to be poor, jobless and in ill health were hardships many local people had to endure. If the breadwinner of the family fell ill or sustained an accident at work and was absent for any length of time, then no money came into the household. If death occurred and money was not available for the burial, then it was the dreaded 'Paupers Funeral'.

It was to overcome this ignominy that compelled many workmen to join a Friendly Society. For a few pence per week they were assured of a grant towards the cost of the funeral, and a small income if they were off work through sickness or an accident. One such society, that had its roots in Ashton under Lyne, and founded in 1826, was steadily spreading its branches throughout Britain. On March 29th, 1899 The Loyal Order of Ancient Shepherds Friendly Society opened a lodge in Southwick.

Their meeting place was in the Sun Inn in Southwick Road.

At the first meeting 24 members were enrolled by the appointed secretary Peter Inglis who lived in Abbay Street. The membership quickly increased as word spread about the advantages and benefits of being in such a society. The vast majority of members being recruited from the shipyards and Wearmouth and Hylton Collieries. By the 1930s the Society at Southwick was thriving.

Local dignitaries were made honorary life members. Among them was the vicar of Holy Trinity the Rev E.W. Bolland (1924), Doctor W.A. Carruthers (1930) and the most recent being the Rev John Troop of St Columba's (1995).

*The fifth and present secretary Arthur Turnbull has held that position since the death of his uncle Frank Turnbull in 1962.*

### First Class!

In April 1935 a report appeared in the *Echo* of the achievement of 61-year-old Mr T. Fenwick of Frank Street. He rose from a pit lad cricketer to a well known first class umpire. He began his umpire career at the Wearmouth ground in 1906, and progressed to umpire many first class county matches. Mr Fenwick umpired Durham v Australia at Ashbrooke in July 1921.

1935 – Mrs Mary Burke of 19 Nelson Street, won the best decorated house competition in Southwick. The competition was held as part of the Silver Jubilee celebrations of the reign of King George. However, a jubilee day boating trip resulted in the tragic drowning of Francis Loughlin (37) of 17 Pembroke Street. Francis, his brother Larry and four young friends were returning from a motor boat trip up river when Francis fell from the boat into the water. A brave attempt to save him was made by his friend Thomas Smiles, but Francis quickly disappeared under the water and was lost. Francis Loughlin left a widow and four young children.

### Armistice Day

Armistice Day in Southwick was a big event during the 1930s. In November 1933, for instance, it was estimated that 4,000 people took part in the procession and service. The parade formed at The Oval and comprised local organisations, ex-servicemen, war widows and orphans, which were led to the Cenotaph on The Green by Southwick Salvation Army Band. Local clergy conducted the service which began at 3 p.m. and hymns were sung by the choirs of St Columba's and Holy Trinity Churches. Ex-D.L.I. bugler C. Hart sounded the last post and there was

August 10th, 1936 – Unemployed men's children are about to have their tea at their sports day at Marley Pots playing fields.

a wreath laying ceremony and two minutes silence was observed.

George Oliver, the owner of The Savoy Theatre, allowed the use of the picture house for the Armistice Day Service in the event of bad weather. This facility was required in November 1934 when it poured with rain.

In November 1935 Canon H.F. MacNunn, vicar of St Columba's Church, addressed another large turn out for the Armistice Day Service on Southwick Green with some interesting words " … The peace which men died for must not be just a breathing space between wars … We must not let the peace we require be filled with preparation for another war."

October 1st, 1936 – The residents of Ogle Terrace, Low Southwick held a 'Farewell Tea' to mark the event that they were shortly to leave their condemned homes for new council houses at High Southwick (The Squares Area).

February 3rd, 1937 – On this day the biggest crowd ever to watch a funeral at Southwick, estimated at 2,000, turned out for Billy Hogg the popular ex-Sunderland AFC footballer. Billy Hogg was the manager of the Old Mill Inn. Above: The Old Mill Inn in the 1930s.

May 13th, 1937 – The residents of Morgan Street held a Coronation Tea to celebrate the crowning of George VI.

October 1937 – Three young men from Southwick appeared in Court accused of house breaking. When questioned about jewellery and money which had been stolen from a house in Edward Burdes Street one of the youths replied: "I knew my sister was out." A police spokesman explained that there had been a spate of house breaking in Southwick during the previous five weeks, and people were in fear of leaving their homes.

February 1938 – A well known pawnbroker from Southwick appeared in court and was fined £10 – the maximum penalty the court could impose for taking articles in pawn from a person under fourteen-years-old. The severity of the fine was mainly because the pledged goods had been stolen by the boy from a clothes line.

November 5th, 1938 – Mr Harcourt Antell of 7, The Poplars retired from Sunderland Corporation after 51 years service as a glazier. Mr Antell was the Corporation's first boy apprentice and when he completed his apprenticeship was presented with a medal commemorating the occasion as the first boy apprentice. Mr Antell did not lose a days work through illness or any other reason in all of his 51 years service.

August 17th, 1939 – A group of friends went to Easington by motor boat to collect coal from the beach, one boy was left in charge of the boat while the others rowed to shore in a small cobble. The cobble filled with water and a lad called Bute swam back to the motor boat for a tow rope. Bute got into difficulties and 25-year-old George Softley Stubbs of Jowett Square dived in to save his cousin. George was wearing a boilersuit and disappeared beneath the waves. He gave his life for his cousin who survived the ordeal.

## Child Neglect

Three astonishing cases of child neglect occurred in 1937 and 1938 when the children involved were taken into care.

A father was jailed for six months in what was described in court as " … the worst case before the court for twenty-two years." The family had been living in Pallion but had moved to Charles Street, Southwick. The house was described as an "abomination of filth." The smell was so bad that the inspectors had to light cigarettes.

A man and his wife from Clockwell Street were jailed for six months and three months respectively for "wilfully neglecting" their two children. Policemen heard screaming and forced their way into the house. A police sergeant described what he found: "An eight month old baby was tied to a chair with tape fastened around its arms and body. The child was blue and shivering with cold and screaming loudly. Its only garment was a vest and he looked like a living skeleton." The father, who had a drink problem, was asleep in another room and the mother was out.

Another case of neglect came to light when one of two brothers aged ten and twelve "asked for more like Oliver Twist" following a free school meal. Their widowed mother had a drink problem and the family had moved to Southwick from Hendon. The two boys were said to be always hungry at school and were described as "pale and poorly nourished, clad in rags and with boots almost in ribbons and their toes protruding … They were a picture of neglect and misery." The mother was jailed for three months.

## Southwick Carnival

The records show that Southwick Carnival was held as early as 1910, and again in 1919 to create funds for the township's disabled war veterans. However, in 1927 a new committee revived Southwick Carnival, and each year it provided progressively better attractions. By the 1930s the week long carnival was a well organised annual event which raised funds for three Sunderland hospitals.

St Hilda's Brass Band headed processions of colourful floats, and senior and juvenile jazz bands. The 'King and Queen' of Carnival, who were crowned at The Oval, were presented with the Key to the Freedom of Southwick. Seated on their throne and accompanied by their brightly dressed entourage, the 'King and Queen' toured the streets of Southwick where houses and shops were decorated with colourful flags and bunting.

*King Carnival (G. Hendry) is crowned at the Oval on 13th September 1930 by Major F.J. Gilbertson.*

An amusement park was set up on The Oval, and at various venues in Southwick there were baby shows, push ball matches, children's sports, comic fancy dress contests and male voice choir competitions. It was estimated that 10,000 spectators witnessed the climax of the carnival in September 1931 – an exciting fireworks display at the cricket ground.

In 1937 Sunderland Corporation took over all carnivals in the town to organise one big event. The Southwick Carnival Committee decided not to join with Sunderland Carnival and were forced to change the annual event's name to Southwick Fete. The structure of the old carnival, however, remained the same.

The 1938 Southwick Fete was opened on Saturday afternoon, July 9th by a stampede of several hundred youngsters to free rides on Powell's Amusement Park to celebrate the opening ceremony. The Southwick Fete was another success in 1938, but then war broke out!

1

2

3

4

5

6

7

8

9

10

# SOUTHWICK AND

23    "When you go home tell them of us and say for
your tomorrow we gave our today."

# THE SECOND WORLD WAR

11

12

13

14

15

16

17

18

19

20

21

22

1. Norman Wilkinson (1920 - 1978)was awarded theMilitary Medal for bravery. (see page 66)

2. 28 year old Flight Sergt Tom Robinson was a rear gunner - 'tail-end Charlie'. He was based at Oban in Scotland where he met Nancy who was a W.A.A.F. and she worked in communications. During the summer of 1942 they married in Holy Trinity Church, Southwick. About three months later in November 1942 Tom Robinson was killed in action. And to add to this sad tale the first message that his body had been washed up on an African beach was received by his wife Nancy, who was on duty at Oban where they were both stationed.

3. Sergt Arthur Vincent was the first Southwick serviceman killed on active service. He left a widow and two young children at 5 Cicero Terrace. Sergt Vincent is buried in Southwick Cemetery.

4. Sapper James Joseph Monaghan's grave in Cairo (see page 66)

5. Able Seaman Luke Farrer served on Russian Convoys.

6. Capt Sidney Brazier who was later taken prisoner by the Japanese (see page 56).

7. Bob Bambrough (1909 - 1990) of 33 Oaklands Crescent was a survivor of the Lancastria which was sunk by German bombs in the Bay of Biscay off St. Nazaire on June 17 1940. There were 5,300 troops and refugees on board and of these 2,800 perished. Bob Bambrough became a sergeant in the R.E.M.E and was a member of the British Expeditionary Force when the Lancastria went down.

8. Lieutenant Jack Bambrough, whose parents lived at 33 Oaklands Crescent, was killed in action in July 1943

9. William Walter Thwaites of 9 John Street (now Darwin Street) won his wings in Ontario, Canada in June 1942. He was stationed at Benchazi, Egypt with 47 Squadron and promoted to Flying Officer. On 15th November 1943 Flying Officer Thwaites was posted missing presumed killed in action over some Greek Islands. His body wasn't recovered and consequently his mother did not accept his death and waited for him to come home. So strong were her feelings that he would return that she made a provision in her will for his share of the inheritance which consisted mainly of her home. Mrs Thwaites died in 1960.

10. Sergt George Atkinson, 100 Maplewood Avenue, worked on bulldozers to construct roads in the jungles of Burma. He is pictured in 1943 aged 20 years while on leave in Calcutta.

11. Edith Ridley (1915 - 1993) of 10 Elmwood Avenue was a nursing sister who joined up as an officer at the outbreak of war. She served with Princess Mary's Royal Air Force Nursing Service and was among the first nursing staff who went to France after D Day. She was awarded the 1939-45 Star, France and Germany Star, Defence Medal, War Medal and Belgian Liberation Medal. Edith was engaged to be married but sadly her fiancé was killed in the war. She never married.

12. Edith Ridley's sister, Ethel (Mrs Patrick), was a midwife based at Murton Street, Sunderland when war broke out. Ethel too, was a nursing sister and joined up as an officer with the Queen Alexandra Army Nursing Service. She served in Iran where she was temporarily blinded from a head injury she received after being jolted out of a wagon. Ethel served in field hospitals and followed the Allied advance around the Mediterranean.

13. Norman Warne (18) died of burns received in action while serving on board HMS Warspite in June 1941. (see page 64)

14. Cabin boy Johnny Banks aged 17 from 2a Park Terrace was lost at sea in 1945

15. The grave of Matty McGough who died in Japanese hands (see page 57).

16. Leading Steward Frankie Bland (25) from Maplewood Avenue was killed in action on a mine sweeper in the North Sea in June 1941. His wife was pregnant with their son when he was killed.

17. Capt Tom Davison the son of Davison the builder of 1 Burntland Avenue, was awarded the Military Cross.

18. George Taylor MBE, GM, Lloyd's War Medal for Bravery at Sea (see page 65).

19. Flight Sergt. Fred Davis (RAF - South East Asia Air Force) aged 23 of 18, Tennyson Street was a veteran of thirty operations with Bomber Command over Europe. When the war in Europe ended he was transferred to India to prepare to fight the Japanese. On June 12th 1945 his plane crashed near Calcutta killing all on board. His wife was pregnant with their second child. After the war Mrs Davis and her two young daughters moved to Bristol to start a new life.

20. Sergt John E. Girdwood (21) of 1, Kertch Street who was on a Lancaster Bomber was killed in action on June 8th 1944 over a target area in France.

21. Henry Lennon – Leading Aircraftman, who died of smallpox in India in 1943, aged 37.

22. Gunner Norman Beadle (22), Maritime A.A. of 39 Edward Burdes Street was killed in action at sea in January 1942.

23. Jossy Wilson, Secretary of Southwick Social Club lays a wreath at the Cenotaph on behalf of the members of the club on Remembrance Sunday 1991.

# INTRODUCTION

After the First World War and during the years leading up to 1939 Southwick had changed. The former township had become part of the Borough of Sunderland, and the events in Southwick's history became submerged and hidden within the history of the town. Robert Thompson's, Swan Hunter's and Priestman's shipyards had closed. So too had Southwick Bottleworks. Almost all of Low Southwick had been demolished and the population were re-housed in new council houses to the north of The Green. There had been the mass influx of newcomers when whole streets full of families were re-housed on the Marley Pots Estate from slum clearance areas of the east end of the town.

No less than 365 Southwick men lost their lives during the slaughter of World War One. A phenomenal number for a place the size of Southwick which claims to have sent more men to war in proportion to its population than any other place in the country. The suffering of the wounded in Southwick was a stark reminder of the reality of war to a new generation of Southwick youth that was growing up in the 1920s and '30s. They included veterans like Hugh Smyth of Oaklands Crescent, Marley Pots who had been severely wounded at Ypres and died in November 1933; and John Joseph Keefe (49) of Sunderland Road who had been severely gassed and died suddenly in June 1940. There was 52 year old Fred Rosebury of Chestnut Crescent who had worked for only a few months since he returned from France in 1918. He died at his home in December 1941. And Robert Swinburne (49) of Morgan Street who died in December 1942 as a result of wounds he received in the 'Great War'.

Indeed, some of the sons of men who died in the First World War like William James, son of Reuben James; Tom Robinson, son of Tom Robinson; and Sam Cawood, son of Gunner Cawood are among the Southwick men who lost their lives in World War Two.

To those of us born later World War Two is only a story, and to those who went to school in the 1950s and early '60s the war was sometimes too near an event to have been taught in history lessons. However, the Second World War is well written and well read history and it is gradually slipping beyond living memory. Such men as Churchill, Montgomery and Eisenhower became household names and are synonymous with the war. The individual deeds of heroism and self sacrifice by Southwick men and women, however, appear to have been forgotten. There were absolutely dreadful experiences for Southwick men who languished as prisoners in Japanese hands. In Southwick there was rationing, shortages and the fear of air raids and death. Long hours were worked by industrial soldiers who fought the Battle of the Atlantic in the shipyards, as well as carrying out duties such as fire watching and service in the Home Guard. Southwick children too, did their bit by organising fund raising activities in an unprecedented war effort. Despite the hardships there developed a unique camaraderie and neighbours helped each other.

To preserve memories of what occurred during 1939 to 1945, I have recorded the names of Southwick men who lost their lives, and of those who were prisoners of war; and some of the events which involved Southwick people. It is hoped that this chapter will give a deeper and more profound understanding of the experiences of Southwick people during World War Two. Lives and education were disrupted and civilian careers wrecked. Six years of youth were lost, and many, of course, paid the ultimate price for serving their country.

*To the Brave Men of Southwick*

# EVACUATION

*Children from High Southwick Junior School in October 1939, who were evacuated to Cowesby Hall near Thirsk.*

The main aim of the National Evacuation Scheme was to remove the Nation's children from congested, dangerous urban areas which might become targets for mass bombing. The scheme was voluntary and the *Sunderland Echo* reported that in September 1939 7,910 Sunderland children went to reception areas in the East and North Ridings of Yorkshire and South Durham. Among this number Southwick children from St Hilda's School were sent to Redmarshall in Stockton Rural District; St Columba's and Grange Park Schools to Driffield Rural District; and High Southwick and West Southwick Schools to Thirsk.

The second evacuation took place in November 1939 when 379 Sunderland children were sent out; and the third evacuation in July 1940 took another 1,761 children away from the danger zone. This total of 10,050 children did not take into account the large numbers whose parents made their own arrangements for seeking safety for their children.

The allocation of evacuees was haphazard, which caused problems. There were class and cultural differences caused by the mixture of town children with country folk.

The anticipated mass bombing of Sunderland did not happen during the 'Phoney War' and there was discontent among parents separated from their children. Moreover, many children were unhappy and there was a continual drift back home.

By November 1940 3,700 children were still evacuated to the country, most of whom had been away for more than twelve months. The *Sunderland Echo* wrote that by June 1941 7,504 had returned home leaving 2,546 in reception

areas. However, there was a constant coming and going of evacuees when some parents registered their children, who had returned home, for new evacuation schemes. On July 2nd 1941 a fourth evacuation took place when 200 Sunderland school children, which included numbers drawn from all of the Southwick schools, left by train for the rural district of Bedale, Northallerton, Leyburn and Malton. This party included a large number of children who had been evacuated before.

There were efforts by Sunderland Education Authority to relieve the burden of separation by periodically putting on special trains and buses at reduced rates for visits by parents.

By Christmas 1941 only twenty-three children from Grange Park and St Columba's Schools remained in Driffield, East Yorkshire out of a total of 400 evacuated to that town soon after the outbreak of war. A Christmas party for the small Driffield community of evacuees was

---

**Memories of Evacuation by Jim Weatherill**

On September 2nd, 1939 I was evacuated to Yorkshire with a multitude of school children. I was thirteen-years-old and I was billeted with a family called Boynton in the village of Pickhill.

The next day on Sunday morning I sat with the family to hear Chamberlain's speech and the declaration of war. The wireless was accumulator powered.

The conditions were, indeed, much more primitive than at home at 20 Dean Terrace. There was no electric or gas light; no water on tap; no flush toilet; lighting was by oil lamp; cooking was by coal fire and primus stove. Drinking water was carried in pails from a spring which ran into a beck ( a stream which ran through the middle of the village green). Washing water was obtained from a hand powered pump which needed priming to get it going. The family also kept pigs and poultry, and ferrets for catching rabbits.

One morning early in 1940 it had been snowing and my friends and I were in the churchyard. We heard a heated argument nearby between two local men. One of them suddenly picked up a long handled spade and began hitting the other repeatedly with it, who in turn ran away. In the afternoon the beaten man returned with a shotgun and laid siege to his enemy's farmhouse. Numerous shots were fired and I could see the siege from the Boynton's house which was about 100 yards away on the other side of the village green. It was like something out of a western film. The police eventually arrived and arrested the gunman who was later jailed.

organised by Sunderland school teacher Miss Jean Luckley who had received a generous response in Driffield for food and funds.

The *Sunderland Echo* recorded that by October 1943 about 800 children from Sunderland were still evacuated. About 1,000 had returned home over the previous ten months.

Some of the evacuated children had become a problem for social workers. At the Annual Meeting of Sunderland Council of Social Service in November 1943 Miss E.M. Carter, the Welfare Officer reported: "No matter how poor the homes of those children who had been left in the danger zones there was a grounding of fundamental principles taught by parents that children who had been evacuated were now beginning to show they lacked. A child felt the need of its parents and no matter how well evacuated children had been treated they all wanted to go home … "

In October 1944 the Government responded to the Allied advances in Europe, which had eradicated the air raid threat, by asking local authorities to make arrangements for the return home of children evacuated with government help. On November 26th 1944 all the remaining evacuees, about 180 children, returned to Wearside.

Out of 24,500 children in the evacuable area of Sunderland 12,000 were registered for evacuation. 10,050 were actually evacuated but only about 180 remained in reception areas until the danger had passed.

*In September 1940 a seavacuee liner - City of Benares - was torpedoed and sank after dark in the Atlantic 600 miles from land, and in heavy seas. On board was a party of eleven children from Sunderland who were seeking safety in Canada. Only two of the Wearside children survived - Eleanor Wright and Billy Cunningham-Short. The sinking was described as the "Massacre of the Innocents."*

*Brothers Billy Cunningham-Short (9) and Peter Short (5) of Hylton Lane were the sons of a Southwick woman. Both boys were believed lost on the City of Benares. Mr and Mrs Short, however, received a telegram which said that Billy had survived after spending eight days in a lifeboat. Mrs Short was overwhelmed - "a miracle has happened!" she exclaimed before collapsing. Peter was lost at sea and the first thing Billy said to his parents when they collected him at Glasgow was: "Mammy, I have not got Peter for you."*

*Derek Leigh, aged 11, of 7 Vedra Street, Southwick lost his life on the City of Benares. He was the son of a miner and the youngest of four brothers. Derek was a boy scout and a pupil at High Southwick Boys School.*

# BLACKOUT

The compulsory period of darkness introduced as a precaution against air raids required the co-operation of everybody. The attitude of some people, however, was sometimes one of indifference, or carelessness, or complete disregard for the safety of others.

During the opening weeks of the war there were complaints of houses in Southwick with no blackout at all, and in October 1939 'Hawkeye' wrote to the *Sunderland Echo* - "Anyone desiring to see the Southwick illuminations can do so any night of the week if they care to walk down the road from Southwick Cemetery after dark. At least four houses in Marley Crescent leave the lights of their windows fully exposed to view and have done so for the past three weeks."

Air raid wardens were kept busy and those in breach of blackout regulations were reported and dealt with in Court. In December 1939 the case of Mary C. of Cato Street who pleaded guilty to failure to obscure a light at her home was dismissed with a caution. At this time fines were varying from 10 shillings (50p) to a £1, though in April 1940 Edith W. of Dryden Street was fined £2 for showing a light during blackout hours. And what was described as " … the most shocking case we ever had before us," Sunderland Magistrates dealt with Mr A. of Knox Square in July 1940, who appeared in court for the second time within a fortnight for failing to obscure a light at his home during the blackout. During an emergency Mr A. allowed a light to shine and when neighbours complained he turned the light off but became abusive. Five minutes later he put it on again. A crowd gathered and were threatening him with violence. Mr A. switched the light off again, and air raid warden George Hall reported that for about 10 minutes Mr A. used abusive language to all that had gathered outside of his house. Mr A. was sent to prison for one month.

Although £2 fines for breach of blackout regulations at homes were regularly imposed, unscreened hand torches were penalised by 10 shilling fines. And in November 1943 Mr M. of Keats Avenue was fined £1 with 4 shillings (20p) costs for using a torch with an aperture of more than 1 inch in diameter in the street during the blackout.

Striking matches in the street during a night alert was also liable for prosecution as two Southwick soldiers home on leave found out in September 1941 at Sunderland Police Court. Isaac Drinkald (29) of Marley Crescent and John George Drinkald (19) of Maplewood Avenue had been drinking and were said to have had a cheeky attitude to the warden who remonstrated with them. In court Isaac Drinkald remarked - "A one armed man asked us for a cigarette and we gave him one and lit it for him." Both soldiers were fined 5 shillings (25p).

Fines of £5 were imposed on individuals who allowed lights to shine from industrial or business premises.

By November 1941 after more than two years of war the Mayor, Councillor Myers Wayman, called for more serious action against offenders because of the continued carelessness in regard to blackout regulations. And 'Ridley Street' in a letter to the *Echo* urged wardens to "get busy" and "… While passing through High Southwick Estate during a blackout I witnessed more lights than Blackpool illuminations ever

displayed. There were chinks in window blinds and a lighted bus which travels up and down during alerts is an open target endangering the lives of hundreds of innocent people."

Despite a 20 m.p.h. speed limit imposed during the blackout the number of fatalities or injuries on British roads during the war were substantially in excess of all British military and air raid casualties combined! Blackout hours increased the death toll especially among the old and very young. It was difficult to spot approaching vehicles with dimmed headlights and internal lights blacked out. 63 year old John Hockridge of Carley Road was knocked down and killed by a bus near his home during the blackout early in 1940. He was one of 28 fatalities on Sunderland Roads in 1940. 12 of these deaths occurred during blackout conditions. There was 82-year-old Thomas Chapman of Ellis Square who was knocked down by a tramcar in Fawcett Street on December 27th 1941 during the blackout. Mr Chapman said that he thought the tram was farther away than it was. He died of shock two days later. There were 27 deaths on Sunderland roads in 1941. 17 of the deaths occurred during the blackout. And there was 12-year-old Gordon Wilson of Church Street who had gone to buy sweets in the blackout and was knocked down and killed by a bus in January 1943, at the junction of Sunderland Road (now Southwick Road) and Carley Road. Gordon was one of six children killed on Sunderland roads in 1943. There were also 11 adult victims in 1943.

In February 1942 the blackout was responsible for the death of civilian war hero 49-year-old Robert Stephen Ward of Yewtree Avenue. In November

*Sunderland Echo* January 5th, 1944

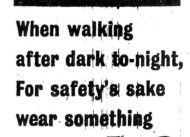

*Sunderland Echo 1st January 1941.*

1941 he was decorated with the British Empire Medal for gallantry. Mr Ward was a yard inspector for the L.N.E.R. Company at Tyne Dock, and during an air raid incendiary bombs were dropped among 300 wagons, some containing ammunition, at railway sidings, setting fire to some of them. Mr Ward and other railwaymen risked their lives and worked among the blazing ammunition wagons.

They eventually moved 274 of the wagons to safer sidings. During the task high explosive bombs fell all around them but all of the men escaped unhurt. On February 12th 1942 Mr. Ward stepped off the pavement in North Hylton Road in front of a R.A.F. bus travelling at 10 m.p.h. and was killed. At the inquest the Coroner told Mr Ward's daughter, Mrs Edith Gibson of Elmwood Avenue "- You have lost a good father and the country has lost a hero."

*Robert S. Ward B.E.M.*

Crime and violence increased on the streets of Sunderland under the cover of darkness. The 'razor and knuckle-duster gang' was responsible for serious assaults during blackout hours. In July 1941 the gang attacked two Southwick men in the town centre and cut one of them. Three eighteen year old youths were arrested and each sentenced to three months imprisonment at Sunderland Police Court. The two Southwick men had been threatened about giving evidence. So seriously were the threats and rumours taken that one of them had actually left the town because of the incident.

There was the 'Sunderland blackout gang' which assaulted timid people in the blackout in the West End of the town. The gang were also responsible for shopbreaking and shouting and

brawling in an air raid shelter during an alert. In January 1942 two of the youths were dealt with at Sunderland Quarter Sessions, and sent for Borstal training for three years.

The arrest of a housebreaking gang from Southwick in January 1943 put a stop to a series of burglaries in and around the Southwick area. The theft of money and goods (which were sold) from houses, and a particularly mean theft from a house in Newcastle Road on Christmas Day, had been spent on drink by the youths in local public houses over the Christmas and New Year holidays.

The names of the same young men from Southwick responsible for housebreaking, shopbreaking and anti-social behaviour repeatedly cropped up in the *Sunderland Echo* during the latter part of the war and post war years. - In October 1944 a gang of 'roughs' were making a nuisance of themselves by jumping on and off the rides on a travelling fair at the Oval. When the youths were approached by the owner and his son, both were assaulted and subjected to abuse and foul language. A 23-year-old Southwick man of Shakespeare Street eventually got on top of the owner's son and gnawed off one third of his ear, permanently disfiguring him. In what was described by the Recorder as an "un-English offence", the man was sentenced to 12 months with hard labour.

Southwick became the Borough blackspot where gangs were a menace to the community. Residents were afraid to call the police for fear of reprisals by a gang of youths who used the tram and bus shelter on The Green as their headquarters. In November 1946 there was described - "a minor

reign of terror at Southwick" by the gang. And a Police spokesman said "Southwick was the worst spot in the town and every time a new constable moved into the area he was subjected to abuse and cat-calling by these men."

Owing to the Allied successes and the march into Germany the blackout was finally eased. From 17th September 1944 the total blackout which had enshrouded Britain for 5 years and 16 nights was replaced by the 'Dim-out'. This meant that blackout curtains could be removed and be replaced by ordinary peace time curtains and blinds. However, room objects and naked shafts of lights had to be prevented from being seen from the street. 568 Sunderland street lights were lit in September 1944, though there were was no lighting of residential streets yet.

# AIR RAIDS

During the crisis of 1938 Air Raid Precaution Trench Shelters were constructed at the Oval and at Clarence Street, West Southwick. Accommodation was planned for 100 in the public shelter and 524 in the communal shelter at the Oval site. At Clarence Street there was room for 312 'public' and 312 'communal'. The communal shelters were provided for local residents who did not have air raid shelters in their back yards. It was their responsibility to keep the shelters clean and tidy. Public shelters, however, were looked after by the Corporation and they were provided for people caught on the street during an alert.

In December 1939 a letter appeared in the *Echo* complaining about the Clarence Street shelters which were situated beside West

Southwick School. 'First Timer' claimed that despite notice boards being erected to indicate the Clarence Street shelter they were in fact nothing more than holes in the ground and had not been completed. The editor of the *Echo* assured readers that the shelter would be finished as soon as possible.

By May 1940 a public trench shelter had been constructed on The Green for 100 people. This shelter can be seen behind the Cenotaph on page 55 of *Southwick on Wear Volume 1*. A similar shelter for 312 people was dug on Thompson Park.

Volunteer Trench Patrol Officers enrolled for duty at the shelter near to their homes. Their main function was to stop all smoking in the shelters, but they were also responsible "to maintain calm and order; to give guidance, comfort and help in times of stress; to prevent panic and generally to assist the public to stand the strain and discomfort of the waiting hours." The Trench Patrol Officers were kitted out with an armband bearing the initial TP, a helmet and a first aid haversack and water bottle.

Trench Patrol Volunteers could be given a hard time particularly by rowdy youths, and in August 1940 there was reported a serious shortage of volunteers in Sunderland shelters. In October 1940 Mrs L was on duty as Trench Patrol Officer in the Oval Communal Shelter. She spoke to the W brothers for their behaviour and appealed to them to show some consideration for babies and older people in the shelter. Later, Mrs L had to speak to the brothers for smoking. One of them was cheeky to her. After the 'All Clear' sounded the boys' mother went to the house of Mrs L and accused her of

reporting her sons. Without waiting for an explanation Mrs W struck Mrs L in the face and broke her spectacles. Mrs W was fined £2 and 4 shillings (20p) costs by Sunderland Magistrates for the assault.

In November 1940 the name Trench Patrol Officer was changed to Shelter Marshal, and in that month it was revealed that practically all of the public and community air raid shelters in Sunderland were damp. Water was entering the shelters via the roof and walls, and during an air raid the people were forced to leave some of the shelters because wet conditions were so bad.

*Air Raid Precautions being dug at The Oval during the crisis of 1938.*

*ARP Trenches under construction at Clarence Street near West Southwick School in 1938. There was a complaint in December 1939 that this shelter had not been completed.*

In February 1941 twenty-one people from Maplewood Avenue appeared before Sunderland magistrates for taking turf from the Marley Pots football fields in October 1940. The turf was used to place on top of their Anderson Shelters. It appears that many Marley Potters had been digging up the turf causing severe damage to the pitches. Boards had been taken away from the changing rooms and an attempt had been made to hack down the goalposts. The people who appeared in court were those who had admitted to the offence when questioned by a policeman. The case was dismissed but they were all ordered to pay four shillings (20p) costs.

# Sharp Attack On North East
## Whole Family Wiped Out

While Bomber Command was attacking Hamburg and Stettin and the docks at Cherbourg, the enemy made a sharp raid on North-East Coastal towns, in which one enemy plane was destroyed.

The attack was over before midnight, but there was considerable damage to property and some casualties are reported. Mainly the damage was confined to working-class and business property.

Eight people, including five of one family, lost their lives when bombs were dropped on houses in a North-East Coast town. Several dwellings were demolished and a number of others damaged. Apart from those killed, there were several who needed hospital treatment after being removed from the wreckage of their homes.

Other bombs which fell in the same neighbourhood caused neither damage nor casualties. One fell near a cemetery, and another made a crater on some allotment gardens.

The tragic family which was hit by the raid was that of William Hacket, a 41-year-old builder's labourer. He was killed along with his wife, Gladys (39), his 16-year-old son Harry, and two school children, Alice (10) and Thomas (6).

The bomb which hit the house while the family were sheltering under the stairs wrote the last page of a week of tragedy.

The Hackets' youngest child, John, aged 10 months, died last week. He was buried on Saturday. William, a 20-year-old gunner in an anti-aircraft unit in the East Midlands, came home on compassionate leave for his baby brother's funeral.

Relations thought he had returned to his unit on Monday, but his name is given in the official casualty list as killed.

### Not in Shelter

The tragedy of the Hacket family is heightened by the fact that the Anderson shelter at the rear of the house was intact. A relation told a reporter to-day, "Bill and his wife hadn't been in the habit of using the shelter for some time. They were of the opinion that the staircase cupboards were safer unless there was a direct hit. Bill argued that the shelter was as likely to get a direct hit as the house."

In an adjoining house, which was also wrecked, were nine people including a number of children. The house was occupied by Dennis Hogan (45), his wife, Mary (48), Teresa (19), Terence (14), Mildred (12), and Dennis (8). The last-named was killed. His mother and sister, Teresa were injured, and taken to hospital. In the house with the Hogans when the bomb fell were Edward Wilkinson, his wife, Gladys and their two-year-old son, David. Mother and son were taken to hospital.

Rescue squads worked tirelessly to extricate these two families from the wreckage.

### Saved by Shelter

In a neighbouring street four members of another family whose home was demolished, owed their lives to the fact that they were in their Anderson shelter. They were Michael Martin (46), a platers's helper, his wife, Margaret and their daughters, Teresa and Ursula, aged 13 and 10 respectively.

They were trapped in the shelter, the exit of which was covered by wreckage from the house. Mr Martin struggled to remove part of the back wall of the shelter and succeeded with the help of neighbours who set to work from the outside.

Mr Martin and his wife suffered from shock, but the children stood up well to their terrible ordeal and were able to chat about it to-day.

Teresa said: "I heard a loud noise which I thought was a plane flying very low, but daddy knew it was a bomb coming and told us to lie down on the seats. The shelter jumped terribly, and the seats gave way beneath us.

### Glasses Blown Off

"My glasses and my shawl were blown off by the blast. For about five or ten minutes we were trapped. We shouted for help and daddy began to try and remove the back plates of the shelter with his hands. We were glad when we heard voices outside and knew that help was at hand."

Eighteen-year-old Margaret Martin, another sister, was sheltering under an exterior staircase of a house some distance away. "When I saw my home go up in the air," she said, "I felt sure that my parents and young sisters would have been killed. I dashed across towards the shelter and was overjoyed to find that it was intact. I could hear no sound of them, however, and ran for help."

In an adjoining flat was 68-year-old Arthur Ridley, a fitter. He refused to go into the Martin's shelter and was trapped by debris for some hours. He showed great stoicism and joked with his rescuers as they were attempting to reach him.

Two other flats were also demolished, but in one there were no people. Thomas and Margaret Rowell, aged 17 and 15, were in the back street while their father was at work. Charles McKinley, who was upstairs, suffered broken ribs. His wife is at present at Redcar recuperating from a recent operation.

### It Wasn't "All Clear"

A number of other houses in the same district were damaged by bombs. The sole occupant of one was Harry Stonehouse, a plater's helper. "I was in the kitchen listening to the gramophone playing. When they sounded the last 'All Clear' when the bombs fell," he said. "I dived under the table and escaped unhurt, although a lot of debris came into the room. The gramophone stopped!"

On the opposite side of the street Albert Simpson (51), a school caretaker, his wife Sarah, their daughter Mrs Ethel Scott and her two children Brian (6) and Albert (4) were trapped in their kitchen but managed to force their way out unhurt.

In bed upstairs was 82-year-old Mrs Sarah Simpson, grandmother of the children. The outer walls of her bedroom were blown away, leaving the bed marooned on the edge of the floorboards. Her main concern was for a half crown she had left under her pillow.

The only casualty in this house was a pet dog, Trixie, who is missing in the wreckage.

In another house a family named Teasdale were rescued unhurt.

A body recovered from the wreckage and not identified is believed to be that of Norah Hogan, twin sister of 19-year-old Teresa.

Many families are homeless as the result of the raid, but most of them were able to find accommodation with friends and relations. Only 27 persons had to be accommodated at rest centres.

*Sunderland Echo October 1st, 1941.*

*The area where the bombs fell was censored but the district described in the air raid is Southwick. The Hackets' and the Hogans' lived in semis on the corner of Shakespeare Street and Cato Street. William Hackett was not in the house when the bomb killed his family. The Martins lived in Dryden Street. Another two bombs fell in Cobham Square.*

Messenger boys were used during the war to take messages from one ARP post to another, to report incidents and in the event of air raid damage to telephones. Leslie Tate was messenger for Pickersgill's Shipyard ARP, and on the night of 30th September 1941 he visited his friend George Gallagher, who was a messenger at Post 8C which was situated next to Beaumont Street shops. Les came out of the post and was walking along Cato Street when he heard the whistling of a bomb: "I hit the deck," said Les. "When I got up the house on the corner of Cato Street and Shakespeare Street about 25 yards away had disappeared. I was first on the scene and I ran towards the rubble where I heard shouting. I pulled some debris away and released two women. The skirt of one of the women was smouldering and on fire. I pulled it off her but burnt my hand in the process. I then led the pair to safety. More people appeared on the scene and the services took over."

*Fifteen-year-old Leslie Tate.*

Billy Hall was head warden at Post 8C. He was also a foreman caulker at Pickersgill's. He wrote a report for George H. Cook, Chief Constable of Sunderland, to give a special mention to Les Tate and others who were involved in the bombing raid on Southwick at about 10 o'clock on the night of September 30th, 1941. " … Miss E. Tindall; this Lady Warden was in charge of the telephone at Post 8C when a high explosive bomb was dropped about 25 yards away. Along with two messengers, T. Hall and G. Gallagher, she was flung on to the floor. The electric light was put out. Immediately after the explosion she got up and by the light of two hand lamps waited to report any messages. The electric light was reconnected and Miss Tindall proceeded to forward her messages to Report Centre. Two slight casualties were attended by her. During all this she remained perfectly calm and stayed at the telephone until the raiders passed.

After recording a similar account previously described by Les Tate, Billy Hall's report continues "… Tate then reported to the post and asked if there was anything he could do. I would like this boy attached to 8C as a messenger."

"Wardens G. Hall, T. Stubbs and J. McGee were on duty on their respective sectors when the bombs were dropped. They ran to the scene of the incident and after much hard work managed to release four people from an Anderson shelter. The shelter was buried under a heap of debris.

"I also wish to mention a member of the Home Guard, a Mr Gowland, who rendered the wardens a great deal of assistance."

*The Anderson shelter from where the Martin family escaped after a bomb demolished their home in Dryden Street on 30th September 1941.*

*The memorial plaque in Southwick Cemetery bears the names of Irene Mooney and members of the Hackett and Hogan families.*

On Friday August 11th 1940 at 9am 19-year-old Irene Mooney left her parents home at 86 Maplewood Avenue, Marley Pots to visit her grandmother's home at Richmond Street at 'the back of the pit'. The sirens did not sound that day and no-one was aware of a lone bomber above Sunderland. Irene often did some cleaning and shopping for her grandmother and on an errand to the shops at about 11.45 am a bomb dropped near to a railway bridge at the Sheepfolds. Irene was walking beneath the bridge and received the full blast which tore off one of her legs. She died of her injuries two days later. Irene's clothing was mattered in blood and the hospital gave them to her family in a carrier bag. The coat was full of holes, probably caused by shrapnel but it looked as though she had been machine gunned. Mr and Mrs Mooney were deeply upset at the condition of the clothing and Mr Mooney buried it in the garden.

At the funeral Irene Mooney's remains were not allowed in St Hilda's Church or in her home at Maplewood Avenue. The cortege carrying the coffin was only allowed to come to the door and the ceremony took place at the graveside at Southwick Cemetery by Father Pollock.

The lone bomber was brought down in the docks and the young pilot was ironically fished out by a relation of the dead girl.

The information was obtained in an interview with Mrs Christina Ward (Irene Mooney's sister) on 31st March, 1996.

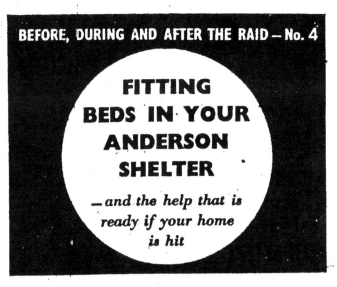

## BEFORE, DURING AND AFTER THE RAID — No. 4

## FITTING BEDS IN YOUR ANDERSON SHELTER

*—and the help that is ready if your home is hit*

WITH very little trouble you can make your Anderson steel shelter a comfortable sleeping place for your family. Four adults and four babies, for example, or four adults and two older children can sleep in a standard Anderson shelter, 6 ft. 6 ins. in length.

All the tools you need are hammer, saw, and pliers that will cut wire. The materials are a few feet of timber, not less than 1½" square, some nails, and some canvas (or hessian, burlap, stout wire netting or similar material).

### QUITE AN EASY JOB

Look at the diagram of the arrangement of bunks and you will at once see the idea. The top bunks run from one end of the shelter to the other, the ends resting on the angle-irons that run across the shelter at each end. These bunks should be 20 inches wide, and about 6 ft. 6 ins. long. The lower bunks are the same size, but rest on the floor, on legs 4 ins. high.

### THE CHILDREN'S BUNKS

The cross bunks for the children are about 4 ft. 6 ins. long, and have four legs each 14 ins. high, which rest on the side pieces of the upper and lower bunks. The cross bunks can be up to 2 ft. wide. The legs must be nailed on inside the shelter.

Fix canvas, hessian, etc., across the bunks and the job is finished. These hints are taken from a very helpful leaflet which is being issued by local authorities to all who have Anderson shelters.

#### SEE THOSE FRIENDS TODAY

. . . and make plans to go and stay with them, or for *them* to come and stay with you, if either of your houses is knocked out.

*Help is ready*
If you can't make your own arrangements and you have to leave your home go to a Rest Centre. Ask your warden where one is. There you will get food and clothes and somewhere to sleep. You will be given advice on your problems and help in finding a new home.

*If your gas is cut off*
There may be a communal feeding centre nearby, where you can get hot meals at very low prices. Find out about it, and if there isn't one, fix up to eat with friends or relations.

ISSUED ·BY· THE MINISTRY OF HOME· SECURITY

*Sunderland Echo 21st November 1941.*

On June 14th, 1941 seventeen-year-old John Mackel of Yewtree Avenue was fined five shillings (25p) at Sunderland Police Court for damaging meadow grass. A bomb had dropped in a field and considerable damage had been done by people tramping down the grass in search of souvenirs.

Although many Anderson shelters flooded in wet weather, the Ridley's at 10 Elmwood Avenue had no such problem. James Ridley was a handy man who installed a sump and field drain to keep the shelter dry. His daughter Catherine Ridley is pictured at the front of the Anderson shelter towards the end of the war. Her father had also reinforced the shelter with concrete blocks and reinforced the door. The tall pole is the family's wireless aerial. In the backyard are the allotments and Old Mill Road.

This World War II ARP surface shelter was revealed in the backyard of a house in Clockwell Street during demolition work in the mid 1980s.

An Anderson shelter in the back garden of a house in Thompson Road in 1996.

# What do I do...

## when I hear guns, explosions, air-raid warnings?

I keep a cool head. I take cover. I gather my family, with gas masks, and go quietly to my shelter or refuge room. I do *not* try to "have a look." I do *not* rush about alarming people. I remember that a lot of the noise is *good* noise — our guns firing at the enemy. And I remember the odds are thousands to one against my being hurt.

**Cut this out — and keep it!**

Space presented to the Nation by The Brewers' Society; Issued by The Ministry of Information.

*Sunderland Echo 5th July 1940.*

The homes of the Fitzsimons' who lived 'upstairs' and the Lynn's who lived 'downstairs' at 1, Wellington Street were demolished during a raid on Southwick on October 11th 1940. Celia Fitzsimons was pulled from the rubble. No-one was killed.

Furniture salvaged from the wreckage of 1 Wellington Street stands on spare ground nearby. A crowd is attracted to the scene. Houses in the background are the rear of The Green. Those to the left are derelict ruins.

The Lynn children who were bombed out of their home. Left to right: Kenneth (2), Ethel (15), George (8) and Margaret (11).

# FUND RAISING

The people of Southwick took part in numerous national fund raising drives for the war effort. These included: The Spitfire Fund, Tanks for Attack Campaign, Warship Week, as well as Wings for Victory Campaign and Salute the Soldier Week. Mrs Crompton and Mrs Bennett of The Green worked particularly hard by organising a series of whist drives in Southwick Conservative Club for the Red Cross POW Fund. The children did their bit too:

*Eileen Collan (12) and Norma Wood (13) of Oaklands Crescent held a jumble sale and made 12 shillings (60p) for the Spitfire Fund in 1940. The girls are pictured handing over a bag of change to the Mayor of Sunderland, Myers Wayman.*

*Two Southwick Girl Guides – Irene Wilson and Martha Stephenson of Beechwood Crescent organised an open air concert in August 1940. They made £3 to help pay for a fighter plane.*

*In August 1940 the children of Camden Street and George Street collected scrap for Sunderland Salvage Scheme.*

*Some children from North Hylton Road held a jumble sale to raise funds for the Spitfire Fund in August 1940. A total of £21,769-1s-9d was raised in Sunderland which was enough to purchase four Spitfires. They were numbered Sunderland I, II, III & IV. The people of Sunderland were presented with a plaque by the RAF for the achievement. The plaque is in Sunderland Museum.*

A concert took place at 13 Dyer Square in May 1942 in aid of Mrs Churchill's Aid-for-Russia Fund. 11s-9d was raised by the organisers Eileen Watson (12), Winifred Sanderson (12), Jean Shaw (9) and Elsie Jenkins (10). The singing and a play was enjoyed by a large number of friends and neighbours.

# The Schneiders

Many Southwick people remember the pork butcher's shop in Southwick Road. Delicious saveloy dips, savory dips, pies, peas pudding, pork dips and cracknel are still sold at the shop today.

Wilfred Taylor ran the pork butcher's business at 231 Southwick Road (formerly 23 The Terrace) from 1934 until he retired in 1970. He allowed the new owner of the business to use his name because of the trade Mr Taylor had built up. In an interview in May 1996 91 year old Wilfred Taylor told an interesting story:-

"Many Germans came to work in England in the pork butchers trade because of the German specialism in sausages. My father, Leonard Schneider, was born in 1877 and he emigrated to work in Wakefield when he was 14. He played rugby league for Wakefield Trinity. My mother, Katerina Kraft was born in 1880 and emigrated to South Shields when she was 17. They both came to England to work in the pork butchers trade. They met in England and married in Gateshead in 1901 when they became naturalised British subjects. My father opened a pork butcher's shop in Gateshead and they had four children. In about May 1915 I was about ten years old and the Lusitania had been sunk by the Germans. My brother, sister and I returned home from the pictures to find a mob from Gateshead smashing up our house and shop which were in the same building. Our parents had left the home and were probably seeking safety at a friends house. We didn't know what to do. A man came out of the house and punched my 12 year old sister in the face. The mob stole all of our clothes but the vicar of St

*The Pork Butchers shop in The Terrace (later Southwick Road) in about 1912. Two names are on the shop front E, F. Lang who sold the business to F. Goetz.*

James' helped us out. The shop remained closed for the duration of the war, but we still lived in the house. It was a strange situation to be in, for, although we had a German name, we were British. My father was called up in 1916 to fight the Germans. When my father was at war a man would come to the house and shout anti German rhetoric which frightened us all. It wasn't a very nice experience when we went for rations and other things and saw some people's attitudes change when we revealed our name.

After the war my father opened up the shop again and traded under the name of Schneider. When we grew up father bought pork butcher businesses for his three boys. He set me up in Southwick in 1934 when he bought the business from Charlie Maurer. I traded under my name Schneider, but we knew war was coming and in 1939 my two brothers and I met to decide about our name. We were not ashamed of our German name or heritage but we did not want our families to experience the persecution we had suffered during the First World War. We

understood that the English equivalent of Schneider was Taylor. So we all agreed to change our family name to Taylor by deed poll. I replaced the name on the shopfront and although everyone in Southwick knew who we were the only trouble we had was when a man knocked on the shop window. I followed him to the Albion Pub and I said I would take him to court, which I did, and he was fined."

*The Pork Butchers shop in Southwick Road in 1996. The shop hasn't changed much and retains its old character.*

# HOME GUARD

Owing to the immediate threat of invasion a plan was formulated in May 1940 for organising the Local Defence Volunteers (LDV). Within six weeks one million seven hundred thousand men, many of whom were trained old soldiers from the first war, rushed to join this voluntary force. Khaki armlets bearing the initials L.D.V. were issued and public appeals were made for shotguns and weapons. Consequently, without uniforms, equipment and weapons the L.D.V trained for an expected invasion in the defence of "their hearth and homes".

By the beginning of June 1940 Sunderland members of the L.D.V. practised shooting at the miniature firing range of Sunderland Rifle Club at Fulwell quarries. In those days there was only one rifle for every eight men.

These were the men of "a great unpaid army" who made considerable sacrifice of their spare time and whose selfless patriotism prompted Churchill to say - " … the Nazis to attempt an airborne invasion would be to descend in a hornets nest."

Early in 1942 conscription was introduced to the Home Guard. Although there were those who thought it was a mistake to apply compulsion to this unique force. The age of volunteers of 17 to 65 was changed to the same as conscription to the Regular Forces of 18 - 51. Maximum periods of obligatory training and duty was not to exceed forty-eight hours per month, but dispensation was allowed to men who worked long hours in industry. The forty-eight hour rule was reduced depending on the industrial demands of Home Guards. The Ministry of Labour was responsible for the selection of men and directing them to units.

After February 1942 Home Guards no longer had the right to give fourteen days notice to resign. And, legislation was introduced for Home Guards who absented themselves from parade or duty without reasonable excuse were liable to a maximum fine of £10 or one months imprisonment or both.

The life of a Home Guard wasn't easy. After a hard day's toil in industry it was tiring to meet the demands of parades three evenings per week, and then sometimes all night manning duty. The regime and discipline was strict - it had to be! A local officer said: "Until the moment when a Home Guard begins military duty he is not subject to military law, but as soon as he begins his attendance on an official parade, then so long as that parade continues he is a soldier with the duties of a soldier, and if

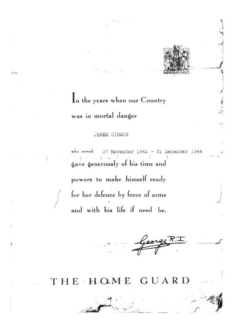

In the years when our Country was in mortal danger

JAMES GIBSON

who served 27 November 1942 - 31 December 1944 gave generously of his time and powers to make himself ready for her defence by force of arms and with his life if need be.

George R.I.

THE HOME GUARD

*Certificate awarded to James Gibson for his service in the Home Guard.*

he offends against these duties he does so at his peril."

Despite the devotion demonstrated by the large majority of Home Guards, there were those who would not attend parades. Like 19-year-old Frederick of Ashwood Avenue, Southwick who had put

in only $7\frac{1}{2}$ hours training since his conscription into C company 9th Battalion Durham Light Infantry, Home Guard in May 1942. In February 1943 he was fined £5 by the Borough Magistrates. It was the first case heard in Sunderland and thereafter absentee Home Guards were regularly dealt with by Sunderland Magistrates. There was John of Jowett Square who was fined £10 in May 1943 for attending only six parades in six months. In September 1943 John was before the Court again for failing to attend six parades since May 1943. He was jailed for one month.

The Home Guard stood down from duty towards the end of 1944 when the threat of invasion had gone.

# PRISONERS OF WAR

At least 106 Southwick men suffered privations and hardships as prisoners of war. Men like Pte Martin Higgins of Wellington Street and Sergt Major George E. Raw of Elmwood Avenue returned home in May 1945 after five years of incarceration. Glider Pilot Sergt Arthur Trueman of 9, Hahnemann Street was another POW to return home to Southwick in May 1945. He was in a group of eight freed prisoners who all lived at Carley Place. Sergt Trueman had been reported killed in action in September 1944. But to the indescribable joy of his family and friends he was 'brought back from the dead', when a postcard was received from him in December 1944 which said he was a POW in Germany and in hospital recovering from wounds.

The quality of life for an allied POW largely depended on where they were imprisoned. When 25 year old Warrant Officer Archie

Donaldson returned to his home in Ridley Street in September 1944 after almost four years of captivity in Germany he was reported to have looked remarkably fit. He said his treatment as a prisoner was "as good as could be expected." And in May 1944 G.E. Judge who served his apprenticeship at George Clark's spoke of his good treatment as a prisoner of the Japanese. For the large majority of Japanese POWs, however, internment was a daily struggle to stay alive, and they were subjected to unimaginable inhumane treatment which has been well documented.

Repatriated POWs had interesting and sometimes shocking stories to tell: Sergt A.C.G. Crossling's family at 14, North Hylton Road were informed in June 1943 that he had been taken by the Japanese. After the war had ended Sergt Crossling recalled some of his experiences: "I was taken prisoner with an American unit in the East Indies. The Japs took us from Amboina to Java. The trip took 66 days and we lost 303 men out of 600. It was hell. We were allowed only half a pint of water a day and as men lay down dying of thirst, Japs actually bathed in fresh water. We worked from dawn to dusk on a diet of rice and water and tea. The Japs put dogs to guard the camp, but they had a bad time - we ate them. We also ate snakes and small alligators and snails."

The starvation diet weakened men's resistance to illness and no less than eleven Southwick men died in Japanese hands. A survivor of the camps was Captain Benjamin Sydney Brazier of Ridley Street who weighed 10½ stone when captured at Singapore. Three and a half years as a prisoner reduced him to an emaciated seven stone. "I was a bamboo man", said 81

*When Warrant Officer Archie Donaldson RAF returned to his home at 72 Ridley Street in September 1944 after almost four years as a prisoner in Germany, his friends and neighbours bought him a cigar case as a welcoming home gift. Above: The eldest resident of the street Mrs M. Ferguson made the presentation.*

year old Mr Brazier at his home in Boldon in May 1996.

Captain Brazier was a member of the 125th Anti Tank Regiment R.A. which was a locally

Captain B.S. Brazier of Ridley St.

raised unit made up almost entirely of Wearside men. The regiment consisted of 602 officers and men who were on board the Empress of Asia bound for Singapore to reinforce the island against Japanese attack. On February 5th

1942 when the troopship approached Singapore it was bombed and abandoned. Although only one of the regiment was killed well over half of them suffered from

Ben Brazier in May 1996.

burns and wounds. Their fighting equipment lost the 125th were issued with rifles and on February 9th were moved to the front line as infantrymen. The order was given to surrender on February 15th 1942 and the Wearside regiment together with 100,000 allied soldiers became prisoners of the Japanese.

405 men of the 125th survived $3^{1}/_{2}$ years of captivity and 197 men died. Of these at least four Southwick men lost their lives out of sixteen Southwick men who were interned from the regiment

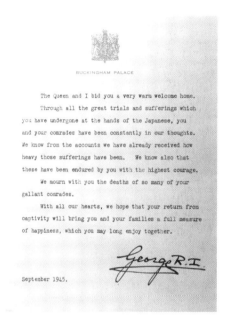

The standard letter from Buckingham Palace was sent to all survivors of the Japanese prison camps. This letter (above) was received by Ben Brazier.

## GERMAN BARBARITIES

# Sunderland P.O.W. tells of Forced Marches

After being forced to march for six weeks from 7 o'clock in the morning until 5 o'clock at night with four potatoes for subsistence the opinion of Sergeant Frederick Feasey, R.A.S.C. (27), of 24 Hawthorne Street, Southwick, that "the German people are rotten," is understandable.

Sergt. Feasey, who was taken at Dunkirk, has just returned to his home and his bitter account of the last weeks of his imprisonment was told to a Sunderland Echo reporter to-day. Only twice during their six weeks' march did they get a quarter of a pound of black bread to eat; for the rest they had to live on the low nutritive value of potatoes.

At the end of each day's march the prisoners were put into barns and specially trained dogs were left outside to see that no man escaped. The men inside were becoming desperate for food, and in attempting to get outside to find something to eat three British soldiers were mutilated by the dogs.

All along the route, evidence of German barbarity was apparent, and dead Jews and Russians lying on the roadway were a common occurrence.

### RECAPTURED

Conditions became so intolerable that Sergt. Feasey and a friend decided to make a bid for freedom. They managed to escape, but had not gone far when they were recaptured and placed in a special camp. Later they were taken to another camp near Nuremburg, and three weeks afterwards Russian slave workers told them that the American troops were near the camp.

Pretending they were ill, Feasey and his friend were left behind when the Germans evacuated the place, and when the Americans arrived Feasey and the other soldier were taken to Brussels.

Sergt. Feasey witnessed one case of the deliberate shooting of a British prisoner. A man from Manchester, named Gribbon, was ordered by an S.S. Guard to fill a barrow with sand, which he did, but when told to wheel the barrow, he protested that he was unable to, and the guard shot him through the head.

Left: Gunner Matty McGough (1, Dyer Square) was reported to have died of Malaria on 30th March, 1945 at Sandakan Camp, Borneo, whilst a prisoner in Japanese hands. The Ministry of Defence records: "After the fall of Singapore several thousand British and Australian prisoners of war were sent to camps in Borneo, mainly on the eastern coast of North Borneo, where they were employed on aerodrome construction... In October 1943 most of the officers were separated from their men and sent to Kuching. Thereafter conditions at Sandakan greatly worsened; the men were starved, beaten and over-worked by their captors. In February 1945 the Japanese, anticipating Allied landings in North Borneo, decided to move the prisoners of war westwards to Ranau, more than 160 miles inland from Sandakan. Although many had been transferred to other centres, more than 2,000 British and Australian servicemen remained to take part in the 'Death March to Ranau'. Those who fell sick, or exhausted on the journey were killed; the survivors who reached Ranau were made to perform superhuman work on starvation rations. Of the 2,400 men who left Sandakan only 260 arrived at Ranau, and most of these succumbed later. Only six survived the end of the war. These six escaped from Ranau and were living with the natives when rescued."

# LIST OF SOUTHWICK POWs

* = in Japanese hands;   ** = died in Japanese hands;   1 = killed while a POW in Italy.

| Name | Rank | Address |
| --- | --- | --- |
| Allen, R.A. | Cpl | Southwick |
| Askew, J. ** | Gnr | 19 Grosvenor St |
| Askew, John * (better known as Norwood) | Gnr | 78 Beechwood Cres |
| Atchison, A. | Pte | Knox Sq |
| Bambrough, J. | Trooper | 33 Oaklands Cres |
| Barnett, Thomas L.G. | Pte | 2 Amy St |
| Bell, A. | Pte | 82 Carley Rd |
| Bell, G. | Pte | 39 Ridley St |
| Bennett, D.C. | Pte | 6 The Green |
| Braley, Harold * | Gnr | 39 James Armitage St |
| Brazier, Benjamin Sydney * | Capt | Ridley St |
| Brown, Joseph Henry | Gnr | 26 Elmwood Ave, late of Keats Ave |
| Bryce, Charles M. | Pte | 35 Beechwood Cres, late of Wellington St |
| Buckley, A | Sergt | 7, The Poplars |
| Burdon, N.T. | Cpl | 16 James St |
| Burlinson, William T. | Stkr P.O. | 16 Cornhill Ter |
| Campbell, E.S. | P.O. | 9 Cobham Sq |
| Clark, Hodgson Raine | Fus | 20 Marley Cres |
| Clasper, A.E. | Pte | 13 Pleasant Row |
| Constantine, E.C. ** | L/Bdr | 11 Beechwood Cres |
| Conlon, George | Pte | 53 The Green/ Wellington St |
| Cook, Robert William ** | Gnr | Camden St |
| Cook, W | Pte | 34 Goschen St |
| Crompton, John R.R. * | Gnr | 30 Wellington St |
| Cross, W.H. | Pte | 26 Dyer Sq |
| Crossling, A.C.G. * | Sergt | 14 North Hylton Rd |
| Cummings, R. | Pte | 68 Beechwood Cres |
| Dobson, James | Sergt | 1 Hawthorn St |
| Donaldson, Archibald | Sergt | 72 Ridley St |
| Elsom, F.D. | Fus | Thompson Rd |
| Feasey, Fred | Sergt | 24 Hawthorn St |
| Ferguson, Donald H * | Gnr | Edward Burdes St |
| Finnigan ** | Gnr | 21 Barnetts Buildings |
| Fisher, J.S. | Cpl | 17 Florence Cres |
| Forster, John | Pte | 22 Cornhill Ter |
| Forster, J.R. * | Cpl | Southwick |
| Foster, R | Pte | 54 Cato St |
| Garrick, John Evan | Gnr | 6 North Hylton Rd |
| Gillis, William | Pte | 19 Carley Rd |
| Glendenning, M | Pte | Old Mill Rd |
| Goldsmith, F | Fus | 12 Clockwell St |
| Gray, J.E. |  | 78 Faber Rd |
| Haddick, Dennis | Trooper | 7 Oaklands Cres |
| Hall, G.F.K. | Pte | 15 Austin Sq |
| Hall, Tommy | Pte | Suddick St |
| Harrison, Arthur | Pte | 81 James Armitage St |
| Henderson, George B. | Sergt | 12 The Poplars |
| Henderson, John * | Driver | 7 Grange Cres |
| Higgins, Martin | Pte | Wellington St |
| Hill, Charles H * | Gnr | 86 Faber Rd |
| Hudson, J |  | Southwick |
| Huggins, Joe * | Gnr | 19 Hollywood Ave |
| Hughes, John | Able Seaman | 7 Beaumont St |
| Jackson, Charles | Pte | Camden St |
| Johnson, J | Pte | 25 James Armitage St |
| Johnson, R | Gnr | 41 Alice St |
| Johnson, T | Pte | Ellis Sq |
| Liddle, E | Gnr | Grey St |
| McGill, Frank | Pte | 12 Pembroke St |
| McGough, Matty ** | Gnr | 1 Dyer Sq |
| Mason, Ernest ** | L/Sergt | 4 Halfway Houses |
| Medcalf, John G * |  | Thompson Park Lodge |
| Middleton, A | Pte | 7 Morgan St |
| Milburn, R ** | L/Bdr | 89 Cowell Ter |
| Miller, J.H. | Pte | 6 Pembroke St |
| Miller, W * | Sergt | 15 Jowett Sq |
| Milligan, T | Sergt | 51 Morgan St |
| Moir, Tom | Able Seaman | 8 Austin Sq |
| Oliver, Arthur | Gnr | 23 Pembroke St, later 6 Hahnemann St |
| Ollerton, Walter | Pte | Sunderland Rd |
| Pepper, S | Fus | 27 Faber Rd |
| Philliskirk, John Robson | Pte | 6 Nelson St |
| Quin, Robert | Pte | 15 Maplewood Ave |
| Raw, George Ernest | Sergt Major | 17 Elmwood Ave |
| Redshaw * | Gnr | 20 Ashwood Ave |
| Roberts, J * | Gnr | 69 Faber Rd |
| Robertson, Wilfrid 1 | Pte | 50 Cato St (Parents Home) |
| Robson, C.E. | Capt | formerly of St Columba's Cottage |
| Rosebury, R. | Gnr | 4 Stoney Lane |
| Rowe, T.M. | L/Sergt | 18 Malaburn Ter |
| Rutter, Thomas P * | Gnr | 5 Fern Ave |
| Sayers, J | Cpl | 8 Clarendon St |
| Shaftoe, T.P. * | Sergt | 75 Maplewood Ave |
| Smith, Joseph * | Gnr | 2 Churchill Ave |
| Smith, Joseph | Pte | Southwick |
| Smith, S. | Pte | 15 Hawthorn St |
| Smith, Thomas * | Gnr | 42 Elmwood Ave |
| Stacey, Malcolm T. * | Gnr | 40 The Green |
| Stamp, Raymond | Pte | Southwick |
| Tennick, G.L. * | Cpl | 5 The Terrace |
| Thurlbeck, Ronald * | Gnr | 20 Oaklands Cres |
| Tonkinson, Sydney ** | Fus | Southwick Rd |
| Trueman, Arthur | Sergt | 9 Hahnemann St |
| Turnbull, J | Pte | 12 Maplewood Ave |
| Tynemouth, Thomas |  | Davison Ter |
| Vincent, Herbert |  | Fitzroy Ter |
| Ward, Arnold ** | LAC | Yewtree Ave |
| Ward, George ** | Gnr | 6 The Green |
| Wardell, Robert B * | Gnr | 8 Hawthorn St |
| Warrener, J | Pioneer | 20 Hardy St |
| Whitfield, J.J. | Pte | James Armitage St |
| Willis, R.R. ** | Gnr | 23 Cowper St |
| Wilson, C | Pte | 32 Back Carley Rd |
| Wood, Robert | Pte | 28 Oaklands Cres |
| Worthy, James | Pte | 6 Branston St |
| Young, Stanley | Pte | 57 Old Mill Rd |

# Heroism, Experiences and Decorations

## RELEASED FROM PRISON CAMP

### Sunderland Seaman's North Africa Ordeal

A Sunderland seaman got "the finest birthday present" of his life on November 8 when in the internment camp at Laghouat, Algeria, he heard over the radio the news that the American Expeditionary Force had landed in North Africa.

He is Able Seaman Tom Moir, whose home is at 8 Austin Square, and he is a survivor of H.M.S. Manchester, the cruiser lost in escorting a Malta convoy in August. Released from internment, he is now home on "survivors leave."

The Manchester was hit by torpedoes from enemy E-boats and so severely damaged that the captain ordered the crew to abandon ship and make their way to the shore as best they could.

"We knew it was internment for us, but that was better than Davy Jones's 'ocker," Able Seaman Moir told a Sunderland Echo representative to-day. "Many of the fellows got away pretty quickly in life boats and motor-boats; but there were about a dozen of us on a Carley float, paddling slowly towards the shore. It took us eight hours to cover the ten miles.

#### LANDED ON BEACH

"We landed on the beach at Beauficha, on the coast of Tunis, and French native troops were waiting to pick us up. There was no welcome—no dry clothes or anything like that, but that wasn't serious since it was so warm. We each got an egg and a slice of bread for a meal before they put us in a prison camp near by. We were there for a couple of days before they took us by train to Laghouat, the internment camp in Algeria, where it looked as though we might see the war out.

"We went by way of Tunis, and the people there seemed very friendly. Many of them ran alongside the train, waving and throwing cigarettes at us. The French guards on the train, too, were very decent; many of them told us that they had fought alongside the British at Dunkirk and were only waiting the chance to do it again.

"Things changed for the worse after Tunis. We were put in charge of the French native troops, many of whom would shoot you as soon as look at you.

"Laghouat was an old Spahi camp, and about 1,000 British prisoners were crowded into accommodation meant for less than half that number. We had 48 crammed into a barracks intended for 24. We slept on plank beds and straw mattresses crawling with vermin.

#### FOOD AWFUL

"The food was awful. It was only the Red Cross parcels which kept us alive. All we got from the French was what they called soup—lentil water with a bit of marrow in it if you were lucky—twice or three times a day, two-fifths of a loaf of bread each per day, a cup of coffee in the morning and a drink of red wine twice a day. There was never any meat, only sometimes a few dates.

"We were supposed to get cigarettes, too, but we had to go on strike—refuse to parade—before we could force an occasional smoke out of them. The French Spahis—Arab cavalrymen—were all right to us. They would chat with us and toss a few cigarettes over the barbed wire, but most of the French native troops were pretty bad.

"One of them pretended he would let one of our lads—Stoker Greaves, of Manchester —escape in exchange for some of his clothes. He took the bribe, waited till Greaves was half-way through the wire and then shot him three times. There was an awful row about that. Our captain refused to accept the apologies of the French commandant, and told him he would have to answer to the British for it.

#### PETTY SPITE

"Actually, it wasn't too difficult to escape from the actual camp if you wanted to do so— but where could you go if you did get free?. You were miles out in the desert without food or water. A few of the lads did make a break but they all gave themselves up again.

"There was no actual physical ill-treatment, but a lot of petty spite on the part of the guards. If they thought we were singing too loud, they would cut off the lights, stop our mail and parcels or refuse to allow us the wireless.

"It was a job to pass the time, but we got up a concert party, played basket-ball and a bit of football when it wasn't too hot. Some of the officers started the 'Sahara University' and ran all sorts of classes in history, economics, literature, and the like. I went to quite a few of the lectures, but I didn't feel able to settle down to study.

"The one wireless set that we were allowed was our great mainstay. Every morning at 6 a.m. and every evening, everybody in the camp would gather round the set in the open air outside the officers' block to listen to the B.B.C. news. The French didn't seem to mind us listening to the news.

"When November 8 dawned, I wasn't feeling too cheerful at the prospect of celebrating my 22nd birthday in a prison camp; but I got the finest birthday present of my life. We were all gathered round the set, straining our ears to catch the news; and when we heard that the Yanks had landed in North Africa, the yell we set up would have roused the dead.

#### FOOD IMPROVED

"The French came running to find out what was wrong; they wouldn't believe us when we told them. All communication with Algiers was stopped, but as soon as they realized it was true you could see the change coming over them. The food improved at once.

"The skipper paraded us and told us that he expected we would all be free in a few days' time, and you would have thought that the cheering would have blown the walls of the camp down. We were freed on Friday, the 13th—what price unlucky 13?—and travelled to Algiers by bus. Coming along the road we passed British tanks and armoured cars and, boy, were we glad to see them! We met the Yanks in Algiers, and we had our first good smoke for ages. It was like walking in a dream—especially when we knew that we were for home right away.

"When I used to stand in that Algerian camp listening to the football scores coming over the radio. I never expected to be back in canny aad Sunderland to see a game this season. It feels real good."

Able Seaman Moir was an apprentice shipwright at Pickersgill's yard before joining the Navy in 1938. The Manchester was the third ship to go down under him. "I wasn't born to be drowned, evidently," he says. He was on H.M.S. Javelin, a destroyer sunk in a fight with German naval forces in the Channel in 1940, and was three hours in the sea before being picked up. He then served on the "much-sunk" Ark Royal from January to November, 1941, when she went down in the Mediterranean.

*Sunderland Echo November 28th 1942.*

*Harry Meadows Langley*

GVI RI

This scroll commemorates

Stoker 1st Class H. M. Langley
Royal Navy

held in honour as one who served King and Country in the world war of 1939-1945 and gave his life to save mankind from tyranny. May his sacrifice help to bring the peace and freedom for which he died.

Harry Meadows Langley from 11 Barrie Square was one of seven brothers. He was lost at sea in June 1940 when HMS Glorious was attacked and sunk by two German battle cruisers. Three officers and forty men were saved of a ship's company of more than 1,200. "Aye, our Harry, we couldn't believe it", recalls his brother Jimmy.

Jimmy Langley (brother of Harry Langley) who served with the Royal Artillery and the Royal Welsh Fusiliers.

"On April 14th 1945 we were advancing in Germany. Snipers were everywhere and I was shot in the chest. The impact of the bullet felt like someone had violently hit me in the chest with an iron pole. I was knocked backwards and I went down. Blood was coming out of my mouth and I was choking. For a few moments I thought that I was going to die. The man behind me got a bullet through the throat. I couldn't stay there and got to my feet. I moved forward for a few minutes but I wasn't sure where I was going. My officer told me to stay put because of the snipers. He dressed my wound and said the East Lancs were following us and they would see to me. They did so and I was eventually admitted to a hospital in Manchester. A doctor said that I was lucky to be alive. The bullet had entered my chest and came out of my shoulder. I had a rough time and they thought I wouldn't survive. The sniper put me out of the war. I'm 74 years old now and I'm lucky to be here today." - Jimmy Langley. Date of interview 6th February 1996.

Sergt. George Laybourn (1902 - 1957) was born in Stoney Lane. He was a member of the 8th Army in the Corps of Royal Engineers and he was awarded the British Empire Medal (Military Division) in recognition for gallant and distinguished service in the Middle East.

*Sergt. George Laybourn's British Empire Medal.*

Peter Longhorn (1899 - 1969) was a well known character who lived on The Green. He served in France as a private with the D.L.I. during the First World War. His service was from February 1915 to November 1919. Between the wars he was in the Territorials but was invalided out of the army in December 1940. During the Second World War Peter Longhorn was Billeting Officer for the North East, and also trained cadets in the evenings. He was promoted to captain and continued training cadets after the war.

Peter Longhorn's daughter, Mrs Farrer, remembers that near to their house at the north west corner of The Green near to the tram terminus was a 'Smoky Joe'. It had funnels and was the size of a lorry. Smoky Joe was lit at night to combine with others dotted around the town to form a blanket of smoke over Sunderland which hindered German bombers. Pedestrians wore luminous badges in the blackout.

RAF Sergeant James Dobson of 1, Hawthorn Street, Carley Place was taken prisoner with the rest of the crew by the Italians when his plane was brought down in North Africa in 1940. He was sent to a camp in Italy where he was a prisoner for more than three years. When the armistice with Italy was signed Sergt Dobson and six friends escaped from the camp and they made a dangerous journey to allied lines. Sergt Dobson arrived home in Southwick in November 1943 but was ordered not to reveal the route he had taken in his bid for freedom. 24-year-old Jim Dobson had been away from home for four years. There had been many changes in Sunderland and blackout conditions made it difficult for him to recognise his home town. Sergt Dobson was later stationed in India where he was murdered and robbed by locals!

Fourth from left with a section of Royal Scots Fusiliers in battle dress is Bob Gibson of James Armitage Street. In Italy in 1943 Fusilier Gibson and a small section of men were cut down by machine gun fire. His widow Nance and brother Pearce continue with the story " … Bob was shot in the neck and the bullet narrowly missed his jugular vein. The rest of the men had been hit in the legs and he was the only one who could walk. He went for help and after walking for about one mile he was weak through loss of blood. A big German sergeant stepped out from some trees and startled Bob. He thought he would be finished off but the soldier said in perfect English that he was giving himself up. He placed Bob over his shoulder and carried him to the Allied lines, which was a feat because Bob was a big man. After Bob had given the location of his section and was treated for his wound he looked for the German sergeant to thank him, but he had been taken away."

John Thomas Bland (1919 - 1995) of 51, Maplewood Avenue was the brother of Frankie Bland who was killed in action. John Bland was a Naval Commando and cox'd landing craft to land commandos. He was involved in the raids on Dieppe and he was decorated with the D.S.M. in May 1942 for his part in the Bruneval raid. (See back cover, top left picture.) In April 1943 John Bland was promoted to Acting Petty Officer.

*John T. Bland's D.S.M.*

William Henry ('Sonny') Scott, aged 19, was drowned at sea when S.S. Stanwold was sunk in coastal waters on February 27th 1941. Sonny was part of a gun crew and is pictured above on the right. He is buried in Southwick Cemetery. Sonny's brother, 11-year-old Brian, had recently went to live with his aunt at Ford Estate after the death of his mother in the January before Sonny was killed. Sonny's death had wiped out Brian's immediate family. His father had died in 1928; his sister Irene had died in 1934 aged 14, and his other brother Gordon had died as a youngster in the 1920s.

# HMS Royal Oak

Harry Howe, Billy Tate and Harry Langley (see page 59) were friends from Southwick who joined the Royal Navy together in 1936. Harry Howe and Billy Tate were on HMS Royal Oak at Scapa Flow in October 1939. On Friday October 13th Harry Howe was moved to a drifter which was a small vessel attached to the Royal Oak. The transfer saved the life of Harry Howe. At about 1 am on 14th October Royal Oak was torpedoed when the majority of the crew slept. Within thirteen minutes she turned over and sank with over 800 men still on board. Billy Tate escaped through a port hole but he received horrific burns. His pal Harry Howe was able to get into the water from the drifter and he survived. Another Southwick man – James Hearn of Yewtree Avenue – was rescued after the sinking.

Mr and Mrs Tate from Nelson Street visited their son Billy at Invergordon. He was able to tell his parents how he escaped. Financial reasons forced Mr Tate to leave his wife Maud with Billy while he returned to Southwick and his job at Pickies. However Mr Tate's workmates collected enough money to immediately send him back to his wife and son. Twenty-one-year-old William Tate deteriorated and died of his injuries on October 27th. It was a particularly tragic blow for Mr and Mrs Tate who had lost two children through drowning accidents. William Tate was the second Southwick serviceman to lose his life in the war, and large crowds lined the streets of Southwick on October 31st to pay their respects, as the Union Jack draped coffin made its way from the Wesleyan Chapel on The Green to Southwick cemetery.

JAMES V. HEARN (survivor)    WILLIAM TATE (survivor)    HARRY HOWE (survivor)

*Sunderland Echo report showing three Southwick survivors from the sinking of HMS Royal Oak (October 17th 1939).*

Harry Howe photographed after the war. He went on to have a long career in the Royal Navy which lasted for 22 years. He rose to the rank of Chief Petty Officer. Harry's brother, Gordon, recalls that he often spoke about his mate Billy Tate and claimed that Billy saved Harry's life because they exchanged jobs prior to the sinking of the Royal Oak. Consequently Harry was sent onto the drifter and was saved.

**FOR BRAVE CONDUCT**

For brave conduct Captain Joseph P. Sidney (30), R.A.C., whose parents live at 14 Beaumont Street, Sunderland, has received the Bronze Oak Leaf emblem which goes with a Mention in Dispatches.

Capt. Sidney, who has been in the Army for 12 years, being on the Reserve when war broke out, rose from the ranks.

*Sunderland Echo October 10th 1944.*

The Koch family (pronounced Cosh), were Germans who lived in Southwick and took out British naturalisation. During the First World War their house windows were smashed. Their son Stanley Koch married Amy Lennon and they lived at 12, South Terrace.

In 1939, fearing a repetition of First World War experiences, the family immediately removed a large brass plate from the door which bore the Koch name. However, the family did not experience any trouble during the Second World War.

## The Southwick Mafia

When Binns was blitzed and burned down in 1940 the total rubble including the damaged stock (and a lot of undamaged stock except for water damage) was dumped in a fleet of lorries running back and forth for about two weeks from Binns to the Marley Potts rubbish tip. The tip area at the time was also being used to train troops in running Bren Gun carriers. We spent hours and hours there hitching trips in Bren Gun carriers and awaiting the next lorry to tip – because by sifting through the rubbish you found the most wonderful things from the burned out store. Tins of foodstuffs, scorched garments, crockery – it was like Christmas for us boys, but then you had a 'Mafia'. The teenagers took control of the tip and elected to themselves first rights to sift the rubble and secured a great haul. Us eleven and twelve-year-olds were left to go through the ash and be lucky with an old cracked cup or saucer. The queues at the Southwick fish shop near Hardy Square in the five shop complex used to be monumental in war time 1940-42. You could stand for an hour. The trick was if the siren went early in the evening alerting for a possible raid the queue in the main shot home quick to get to shelters. From Marley Crescent, where we then lived, we could make it to the fish shop in ten minutes and it was bliss to find the shop nearly empty except for the staff wanting to get rid of the last fry-up before shutting up and joining the shelter crowds.

by John Curtis

When the steamer SS Goodwood was torpedoed by a U-Boat in the North Sea in September 1940, the Captain was trapped in the bridge. Captain Hewson of Sunderland told the crew to leave him and save themselves. However, Lloyds reported: "The second officer saw to the lowering of a boat, but it could not be brought alongside. He therefore tried to swim back to the ship to rescue his captain who was trapped in the wreckage with both legs broken, but he lost his lifebelt and being in difficulties returned to the boat. Volunteers were then called for to go with the second officer to rescue the master. Able Seaman Broderick (of Southwick) and Gill (of Whitburn) swam back with the second officer to the ship. The three of them got the master clear of the wreckage, carried him to the side, lowered him into the water, and swam with him back to the lifeboat."

All twenty-one of the crew of the Goodwood were saved. For this exceptional act of bravery the three seamen who saved their captain were decorated with the Lloyd's War Medal.

*Thomas Broderick of 49 Old Mill Road, Southwick was awarded the Lloyd's War Medal for his part in the rescue of Captain Hewson.*

*Armistice Day Feat*

BOMBARDIER James Newby, recently awarded the George Medal for bringing back a dying officer over a live anti-tank minefield on November 11, 1940, is the eldest son of Mr and Mrs Thomas Newby, of 7 Chestnut Crescent, Southwick.

Bombardier Newby, who, prior to outbreak of war, was an

insurance agent, enlisted at the age of 29 as a volunteer in the anti-aircraft artillery, a month after hostilities broke out. He was made a lance-bombardier a month later and bombardier shortly afterwards.

Bombardier Newby was employed at Wearmouth Colliery as a coal cutter for several years.

His father, at present an employee of Sunderland Corporation Cleansing Department and a member of an A.R.P. decontamination squad, served overseas in the Great War, first in the Durham Light Infantry and later in the Royal Air Force.

Both parents are prominent members of Bright Street Methodist Church, Roker.

*Sunderland Echo March 14th 1941.*

CAPTAIN THOMAS FRASER, of 41 Grosvenor Street, Southwick, who has received a commendation in the latest list of Merchant Navy awards, for his gallant conduct when his ship was torpedoed and sunk last year.

*Sunderland Echo March 21st 1941.*

**Norman Warne**

In March 1941 eighteen-year-old Norman Warne served on HMS Warspite in the Battle of Matapan. On May 22nd, 1941 during the Battle of Crete the Luftwaffe bombed Warspite. Norman was badly burned in the attack. An account of the carnage below deck was recorded by Warspite's executive officer Charles Madden. " ... There was a huge hole in the deck ... from which smoke and steam were pouring out. I ... went down to the port six inch battery ... to try to get at the seat of the fire through the armoured door that connected the port and starboard six inch battery deck ... We had great difficulty in opening the door and had to use a sledgehammer. Finally it gave, to display a gruesome scene. The starboard

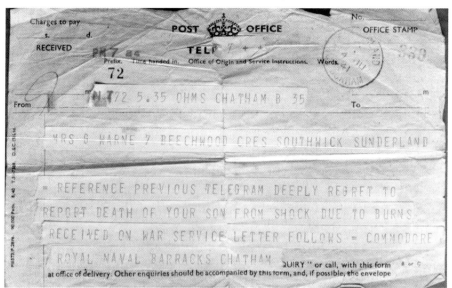

*Telegram dated June 4th 1941 was received by Norman Warne's mother informing of her son's death.*

battery was full of flames and smoke, in among which the cries of burned and wounded men could be heard. This was very unnerving ... I was soon joined by fire parties ... but was hampered by the continued cries of the burned men, which distracted the fire parties who wanted to leave their hoses to assist their comrades. I therefore concentrated on administering morphia ... As it was dark and wounded men were thrown in all directions amongst piles of iron-work and rubbish this was not easy. ... I then went to the starboard mess decks where a fresh scene of carnage greeted me ... When all was in control I went to the bridge to report. The calm blue afternoon seemed unreal after the dark and smelly carnage below."

Norman Warne died in hospital in Alexandria a week or so later.

---

In North Africa in 1942 Sergeant John P. Hetherington of the Paratroop Regiment led a group of men which succeeded in silencing a nest of enemy machine guns. Prisoners were taken and when the paratroops began marching them towards British lines one of the prisoners pulled out a small concealed weapon and killed Sergt Hetherington. His home was at 49 James Armitage Street (corner of Collingwood Street).

*Sergt John P. Hetherington*

Robert Gregory (59) and his 21 year-old son Frederick, both from 49 Cato St., were lost at sea when their merchant ship was sunk in August 1940.

**George Taylor MBE, GM and Lloyd's War Medal for Bravery at Sea.** George Taylor of 17 Grange Crescent, Southwick was Second Officer on board the San Florentino when she was torpedoed and sunk by a U-Boat in the North Atlantic on October 2nd 1941. For his part in the incident (reported right) George Taylor was awarded the George Medal and Lloyd's War Medal for Bravery at Sea.

George Taylor returned to sea and was on board the San Ernesto when he was sunk for the second time on June 15th 1943. A Japanese submarine torpedoed the ship in the Pacific. George Taylor took charge of one of the lifeboats which was at sea for 28 days and travelled 850 miles before being rescued. One of the men died during the voyage and was buried at sea. As a result of the ordeal George contracted malaria and dysentery and his normal body weight of 11 stone was reduced to 6 $^1/_2$ stone. Despite his personal suffering it was said of him: "Displayed good judgement in remaining in the vicinity of the wrecked vessel for 36 hours. Throughout the whole period, by his courage and confident manner, he displayed leadership of the highest order and inspired his men to carry on until they made land." George Taylor was awarded the MBE for the San Ernesto incident.

George died on October 4th 1984 aged 70. A former colleague – E.A. Rogers – wrote in a shipping magazine (Nov. 1984) "… Truly the passing of a little known hero."

*George Taylor was presented with the George Medal by the King at Buckingham Palace. He is pictured with his wife and mother outside of the Palace. His wife Vera, is holding the George Medal. George Taylor later became a captain and then master mariner.*

# Fought U-Boats for Five Hours

For more than five hours, while his torpedoed ship lunged through heavy moonlit seas, Second Officer George Taylor (28), of Grange Crescent, Southwick, stood at the gun and fought a battle against U-boats.

The London Gazette, announced, on March 2, that he has been awarded the George Medal and says his shooting was "magnificent."

For their part in the grim battle against the wolves of the under seas, two other officers and two men of the ship's crew have also been honoured. Chief Officer Stanley Miller, of Brighton, gets the O.B.E. (Civil Division). Third Engineer Leonard Victor Grinstead, of Birkenhead, the M.B.E. (Civil Division), and Gunner Sidney Freeman and Able Seaman Paul Needham have been awarded the British Empire Medal.

Second Officer Taylor is at present at sea, but his wife today told the Sunderland Echo the story of the battle as he had told it to her after the Admiralty had credited him and his shipmates with a hit on one of the U-boats.

"My husband was going to bed when a torpedo struck the ship," said Mrs Taylor. "He jumped into his clothes and reported to the captain, who ordered him to take over the gun.

## KEPT AT BAY

"The ship stood up to the torpedo blow magnificently, and, with the assistance of Freeman and Needham, my husband fired continuously, keeping the U-boat at bay and, for the most part, under water.

"Another hit with a torpedo when their ammunition was about spent broke the ship in two. She started to go down by the middle. The propeller lifted out of the water at the stern, and the bows were raised vertically in the air.

"Orders were then given to abandon ship. Two boats were launched. That which my husband took charge of was all right, but the mate's boat was filled to the gunwhales with water.

The captain's boat had been smashed and could not be launched, so he, with the chief engineer and a number of men, got on to a raft. The U-boat could apparently see the red lights which the men carried on their jackets, as they sat on the raft smoking and joking about going for a joy-ride in the Atlantic in that weather. A torpedo struck the raft and blew them all sky high.

"My husband's boat was drifting about in appalling weather conditions for about 20 hours before they were picked up. The survivors in the captain's raft were rescued shortly afterwards, but better that, nine men had died from exposure.

"Two other men who were rescued had a remarkable experience. One of them was the third officer, a slip of a Scots boy. He and his companion were marooned in the heavy seas, high on the vertical bow of the ship. It was impossible to rescue them. They remained there while shells whistled around as one of the U-boats attempted to sink the after-part of the broken ship with gunfire. They were rescued about 20 hours later.

"I know all the men who have been honoured, through visits to my husband when he has been in port. They are a grand lot of fellows, and I am proud to know them all.

"There were others who deserved as much, but they died. I am thinking particularly of the three wireless operators, George Ward, of Nottingham; Stanley Carpenter, of Wembley; and Thomas Alexander, of South Shields, who remained at their posts until the last, and were killed when the torpedo struck the raft."

The official account of the action, as published in the London Gazette, is as follows: "The ship was attacked by a submarine and torpedoed. For over five hours the two vessels fought in very heavy seas. Later, a second U-boat joined in the attack.

## DIRECTED GUNFIRE

"The chief officer directed gunfire from the monkey-island and, by his skilful conning of the ship and his fine defence control, succeeded in keeping the enemy at bay through the long hours of darkness.

"The third engineer was on watch in the engine-room, and, only with difficulty, was persuaded to leave his post when the ship at last had to be abandoned.

"The second officer was in charge of the gun, and stood to his post throughout the action, shooting magnificently. Freeman and Needham fired under his orders. The three men fought until they had only three shells left.

"Later, the second officer manned one of the falls to lower a boat and, when it was clear, jumped overboard, swam to it, and took charge.

"By his courage and fortitude he kept up the spirits of the tired men until at last they came to safety. Freeman and Needham did good service in this boat."

Second Officer Taylor, who has been going to sea since he was 16, served his apprenticeship with the Silver Line.

*Sunderland Echo March 4th 1942.*

Montgomery is pictured pinning the Military Medal to Southwick man Norman Wilkinson, which was awarded for bravery in the field. The 6th Battalion The Royal Scots Fusiliers had crossed the River Elbe in April 1945. The Citation records "… Lance Sergeant Wilkinson, after disembarking from his craft immediately rallied his section and personally led them to the top of the quarry where he himself silenced the Light Machine Gun post taking all the post prisoner. The 20mm gun had still to be overcome. After a quick reconnaissance Lance Sergt Wilkinson again led his section in a bold and courageous attack around the flank onto the enemy position. With complete disregard to his own personal safety he led the assault and captured the 20mm gun intact with all its crew …"

Norman Wilkinson's bravery allowed following troops to cross the river without the risk of casualties. He died in 1978 aged 58 after spending the last eight years of his working life at Austin & Pickersgill's shipyard. He was formerly a miner.

*Below: Both sides of Norman Wilkinson's Military Medal.*

Above: Sapper James Joseph Monaghan of 40 Oaklands Crescent had an enthusiasm for motor bikes and became a dispatch rider with the Royal Engineers. On the 18th August 1941 25 year old Spr Monaghan was shot by a sniper and he fell with his bike into the Suez Canal. He is buried in Cairo.

# The Evans Brothers

*Billy Evans*

*Tom Evans*

Billy and Tom Evans were the sons of a miner who had moved from a small village in North Wales to work at Wearmouth Colliery. The family lived at 14 Frank Street for many years. Billy and Tom were good sportsmen and played cricket together for Wearmouth in the Durham Senior League during the 1930s. They both played football (see page 9). Billy played top class amateur football for Bishop Auckland, and was a member of the successful team of 1938-39 with Bob Paisley when they won the FA Amateur Cup, the Durham Challenge Cup and the Northern League. The War drastically changed the fortunes of the Evans brothers. Billy was called up and he became a paratrooper. He took part in the Battle of Arnhem in September 1944 when the Allies were met unexpectedly by a strong force of crack SS Panzer troops. His son Dr David Evans continues with the story: " ... Cpl William Evans landed in the first glider to touch down on the drop zone at Oosterbeck to the west of Arnhem. There followed an advance of almost seven miles to the Arnhem

bridge itself. His was one of the units to cross the bridge against heavy opposition. They held that position for eight days. William was badly wounded by shellfire on the last day. He suffered blast injuries to his right side, a shattered right shinbone and the loss of his right eye. Too badly injured to be moved he was left behind as his remaining comrades withdrew, some swimming the Rhine to safety. He thinks he lay for two days before being rescued by a party of Dutch nuns from the local convent who were searching the battlefield for survivors. He was taken to their makeshift hospital and cared for until he was collected to become a prisoner of war.

"After time spent in prison hospitals and holding camps he was judged fit to transfer to Stalag VII B in Bavaria. It was a four day journey through the German winter crowded in a cattle truck. The time he spent as a prisoner of war was one of great hardship and discomfort which it would take him many years to get over. The camp was eventually relieved by the advancing American forces and

after a rail transfer to Belgium William returned to England. He required a lot of medical treatment and assessment before his final discharge and the return to civilian life was not easy.

"Any further involvement in sport was prevented by his injuries, but he remained an active supporter and member of the Wearmouth Cricket Club for many years."

Eighty-one-year-old William Evans now lives near his son David at Whitley Bay. Billy's brother Gunner Tom Evans was accidentally killed in the Middle East in June 1943 aged 30.

---

### Killed in Action

News has been received that Ninian Lyle McFarlane, Sub-Lieutenant Engineer, R.N.V.R., youngest son of Mr and Mrs R. O. McFarlane, of 17 Trinity Street, Southwick, has been killed in action at sea.

ENG.-SUB. LIEUT. McFARLANE

Mr McFarlane served his apprenticeship with Sunderland Forge and played in the Apprentices' League. He was a member of the team that won the North - Eastern Apprentices' Shield. Bob Wood became interested in him and got him to sign forms for Sunderland and he did his training at Roker Park in the evenings.

After completing his apprentice-he had trials for Horden Colliery in the North-Eastern League and played a number of games for Shildon Colliery. He gave up football for the sea, and at the outbreak of war was serving as Junior Engineer with Shaw, Savill, Co. He left to take a Commission in the Royal Navy.

When at West Southwick School he played football for the school, and also appeared for the Town Schools' cricket eleven.

*Sunderland Echo August 22nd 1941*

# PICKED UP BY A SUBMARINE

## WEARSIDER'S DRAMATIC EXPERIENCE

## DAYS AND NIGHTS ON PATROL

When a cargo ship was torpedoed and sunk by a U-boat in the Atlantic the crew of 43, including a Sunderland man, had the strange experience of being picked up by a British submarine which continued her underwater patrol for several days before landing them at a p rt.

The Wearsider, Mr David Cromble, (40), a gunlayer, of Morgan Street, Southwick, told a thrilling story of his experiences to a Sunderland Echo representative to-day.

"Our ship was struck by a torpedo from a U-boat," he said. "Although the vessel began to founder the crew were remarkably lucky, as not a single man was hurt.

"Before the ship went down we managed to send out an S.O.S., giving our position. Then we launched the boats without mishap and cruised around waiting for a rescue ship to arrive.

"Next day we sighted a surface submarine on the horizon and when it made towards us we concluded that we were to be taken prisoner. It was a most disagreeable prospect, even when one is in an open boat in the middle of the Atlantic.

"You can imagine our relief when we discovered it was a British submarine. The commander of the submarine asked us if we wanted a 'lift,' and he soon got his answer.

### "FINE LOT OF FELLOWS"

"It was a rather unnerving experience to go aboard her. When she submerged I had a few horrible moments, but it was surprising how soon we got used to it, though I suspect that none of us was ever really comfortable and we were all glad when the strange voyage was over.

"We spent several days and nights on patrol in the submarine, which was a great deal of the time under water. It was, fortunately, a patrol without incident so far as we could ascertain.

"The officers and crew were a fine lot of fellows and did all they could to make us comfortable and to keep us entertained. We most missed our cigarettes when the ship was submerged.

"Sleeping accommodation proved one of the biggest problems, as a submarine does not claim to be the Queen Elizabeth and has few 'spare bedrooms.' We just had to stow ourselves away where we could find a vacant corner and make the best of it.

"Most of our time was spent in playing cards, draughts, and dominoes, and in listening to the ship's gramophone. We could not quite overcome the strangeness of the life, but it was surprising how we settled down to our surroundings."

Earlier in the war Mr Cromble was on a ship which was bombed and machine-gunned by enemy aircraft in the North Sea.

*Sunderland Echo September 4th 1941.*

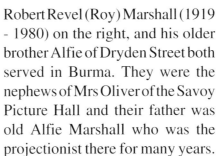

Robert Revel (Roy) Marshall (1919 - 1980) on the right, and his older brother Alfie of Dryden Street both served in Burma. They were the nephews of Mrs Oliver of the Savoy Picture Hall and their father was old Alfie Marshall who was the projectionist there for many years.

Right: Roy Marshall's Burma Star.

While Roy Marshall was serving in Burma he spent some time in hospital where he sketched some of his experiences. Above: is an incident where he was involved in hand to hand fighting with the Japanese.

Roy Marshall was involved in a few hand to hand skirmishes with Japanese soldiers. On one occasion he took an officer's sword from him. Left: The sword is in the possession of Roy Marshall's son, Alan, who is pictured with it.

Twenty-two-year-old George Gibson was called up in January 1940. In July 1942 he sailed for Egypt with British troops. To avoid U-Boats they travelled down the coast of the Americas and back across the Atlantic to South Africa. Above: George (left) is pictured with his two mates in Durban – Billy Knox of Pelton Fell (centre) and Joe Earnshaw of Leicester (right). Some of the troops continued the voyage to Egypt, while others headed for the Far East and met their fate with the Japanese.

Later George was separated from his two pals who were transferred to the DLI while he stayed with the Lancashire Fusiliers. Joe was taken prisoner and Billy was killed in action on D Day. George Gibson served abroad for four years and he was part of the Allied advance in Italy. He was demobbed in April 1946.

Seventy-eight-year-old George recalled with a wry smile the times he spent with his two mates: "Billy Knox, who was killed on D Day, came home with me once and stayed at 61 Shakespeare Street. He didn't drink much – until he met our Jim!"

Jackie Wolfe and Lizzie Sanderson were married in May 1942. They were typical of many newly married British couples when war service caused years of separation. They are pictured outside of the bride's home at 12 Dyer Square. Right is Jimmy Gibson the best man. On the left is Tot Sanderson – bridesmaid.

## AWARDED MILITARY MEDAL
### EX-SOUTHWICK MAN'S PLUCKY DEEDS

A native of Sunderland, Pte. Norman Pollard, D.L.I., son of Mrs Dora Pollard, of 42 West Street, Leicester, and formerly of Julius Cæsar Street, Southwick, has been awarded the Military Medal for gallant and distinguished services in North-West Europe. He was later reported as missing, believed killed.

The citation announcing the award says: " At Pierre, on June 17, 1944, Pte. Pollard was ordered as a company sniper to cover a platoon of his company during the clearing of a wood known to be occupied by the enemy. The platoon met very heavy machine-gun fire and was compelled to withdraw, leaving behind two badly-wounded men.

Pte. Pollard then went forward under fire and brought back one of the wounded. He also endeavoured to bring in the second wounded man, but was unable to reach him.

As soon as it was dark Pte. Pollard volunteered to try to reach him, and went out with another volunteer, but on reaching the man they found him to be dead. Pte. Pollard's unfailing courage and general conduct were an example to the company."

*Echo July 13th 1945.*

### Pte. Norman Pollard.
*His brave deed with the Durham Light Infantry was eleven days after D-Day. Shortly after he was killed in action.*

### Decorations

| | | |
|---|---|---|
| Bambrough JC | Civilian | BEM |
| Bethel WJB | Sergt | Colonial Police Medal |
| Blair S | Civilian | BEM |
| Bland JT | Able Seaman | DSM |
| Broderick T | MN | Lloyd's War Medal |
| Carlson KE | MN | MBE |
| Carter GM | Civilian | CBE |
| Charlton J | MN | BEM |
| Davison TK | 2nd Liet | Military Cross |
| Farrer J | Ord Seaman | MiD |
| Fraser T | MN | Commendation for Gallant Conduct |
| Heptinstall JP | Sergt | MiD |
| Heptinstall RO | Civilian | MBE |
| Hetherington JP | Sergt | MiD |
| Hodgson TS | Yeoman of Signals | MiD |
| Hopper FW | Civilian | MBE |
| Hutchings A | Able Seaman | MiD |
| Jouana JR | Bos'n M.N. | Gold Medal * |
| Kelsall J | Civilian | MBE |
| Martin JJ | Telegraphist | MiD |
| Mitchinson J | Civilian | For Brave Conduct ** |
| Newby J | Bombardier | George Medal |
| Parry G | | Certificate for Devotion to Duty |
| Pollard N | Pte | MM |
| Sheriff J | Pilot Officer | Distinguished Flying Cross |
| Shonewald H | Cpl | MiD |
| Sidney JP | Capt | MiD |
| Stubbings W | Chief PO | MiD |
| Taylor G | MN | BEM, GM, Lloyd's War Medal |
| Thompson BS | Civilian | BEM |
| Vincent HWJ | MN | Commended for Brave Conduct |
| Ward RS | Civilian | BEM |
| Wilkinson N | L/Sergt | MM |

\* Gold Medal awarded by Sweden for gallantry at sea to John R. Jouana of Marley Crescent who had helped to save some Swedish seaman in 1940.

\*\* A gold watch was presented to J. Mitchinson by the men of Pickersgills shipyard in recognition of his brave conduct during an air raid on Sunderland.

MiD  Mentioned in dispatches.

Ron Giles (left) is pictured in 1995 on the 50th anniversary of the ending of the war. Ron was in the merchant navy and his home was in John Street (now Darwin Street). His ship was torpedoed and sunk in the Indian Ocean in 1944 which included twenty Wearsiders. The crew had taken to the lifeboats and Ron records – "The U-Boat surfaced and then approached our lifeboat. Speaking through a megaphone in perfect English someone asked us to go alongside and asked questions such as name of ship, cargo and nationality. He also asked if anyone was injured and did we have supplies in the boat. He told us our emergency wireless message had been answered. Then he wished us good luck and good bye. After almost two days in the lifeboats we sighted land and eventually came ashore in Portuguese East Africa. The natives were armed with spears and knives but fortunately they were friendly. They were all around us and brought us coconuts to eat and mats to lie on. They also lit big fires for us. It was like something from an adventure book. The Royal Navy eventually rescued us."

## Glider Pilot Home From Normandy

Piloting one of the gliders to land in Normandy during the early hours of D-Day was Sergt. Pilot Robert Whitten, of 26 The Green, Southwick, 23-year-old member of an airborne division which is making a name for itself on the invasion front. He was at home yesterday.

Piloting one of the heavier type of gliders carrying tanks and troops, Sergt. Whitten landed his men near the much-contested bridges over the canal at Caen. His wife told a Sunderland Echo representative to-day that her husband was rather quiet about things, but he did tell them of a rather narrow escape he had.

After landing the glider was left behind and the men proceeded to their positions.

### LEFT FLASK BEHIND

Suddenly someone remembered they had left a flask of tea behind in the glider, and Sergt. Pilot Whitten decided to go back for it.

After crawling through the woods on his stomach he eventually reached the glider and found the flask inside intact. Coming through the door he climbed on to the fuselage and over the nose when, suddenly, he heard a shout from one of the men posted some distance away.

Instinctively Whitten ducked, and as he did so the tail of the glider was shattered by snipers' bullets. But Whitten managed to hold on to his prize and the men enjoyed a well-deserved drink of tea.

Sergt. Pilot Whitten joined the Army when he was 18, and was in the bomb disposal unit of the Royal Engineers. Later he joined the airborne section. Before the war he was a carpenter at J. L. Thompson & Sons' shipyard.

His brother-in-law, Dr William Carruthers, of Southwick, is also serving with the Forces.

*Sunderland Echo June 12th 1944.*

Jim Fletcher worked on Sunderland Trams and lived with his wife Lilian in Keats Avenue at the outbreak of war. Jim joined up and he was at Dunkirk. He was disabled because of the war. Jim and Lil recently celebrated their Diamond Wedding in 1995. Jim Fletcher's medals are left to right:- War Medal, 1939-45 Star, 'For Long Service', Dunkirk Medal (and certificate), Defence Medal.

Industrial soldier Harry Mills of 26 Stoney Lane is presented with an inscribed gold watch on April 10th 1942 – his 80th birthday – by Mr Berry director and General Manager of George Clark's engine works. The award was in recognition of fifty-nine years service as an engineer with the company. Mr Berry described

Harry's attitude to work and time keeping as "something unique", and that he was an outstanding example. Harry said that he was content with a good wife and a good allotment. "My only ambition", he said, "is to live and carry on my job till the work is done and the war is won." Harry also received a letter of congratulations from the Admiralty for his service to the shipbuilding industry.

Harry Mills finally retired from Clark's and left his turning machine for the last time on September 21st, 1945. He was eighty-four. During the whole of the war he hadn't lost a minute through sickness, lateness or for any other reason. The war had been won and Harry had been proud to do his bit.

## Margaret Thompson Park Wartime Nursery

Owing to the large number of local women employed in essential work during the day a site for a nursery for their children was chosen in Thompson Park in May 1943. The foundations were laid in February 1944 and the nursery was opened in September 1944. There were places for fifty children.

Right – Children in the wartime nursery shortly after it was opened. Girls left to right: Norma Batey, Linda Atkinson, Jeanette Petrie (Matron's daughter) Margaret Loughlin. Boys left to right: Edward Mahoney, Edward Wilkinson, Arthur Clarke (standing) Ian Jameson, Michael Gardiner (hidden).

Right – Nursery staff after the war. Back row left to right: V. Coxon, E. Bartram, D. Turner, J. Chapman, M. Bartram, P. Bawn. Front row: Mrs Tiltman, Sister Pullan, Dr Flintoff, Matron Petrie, N. Ridley. Matron Petrie and Nancy Ridley were from the original staff when the nursery opened.

# Roll of Honour

| Name | Age | Rank | Date of Death | Name | Age | Rank | Date of Death |
|------|-----|------|---------------|------|-----|------|---------------|
| Anderson, R | | Sergeant | | Carr, Herbert | 32 | Chief Officer | Jan 1944 |
| Askew, J.A. | 21 | Gunner | Dec 1943 | Cawood, Samuel Arthur | | Trooper | |
| | | | | Charlton, John | 23 | Flight Sergt. | June 1944 |
| Bambrough, John | | 2nd Lieut. | July 1943 | Charlton, William Armstrong | 21 | | Nov 22 1945 |
| Banks, J | 17 | Cabin Boy | | Cobb, Robert Roy | 37 | Second Engineer | |
| Beadle, Norman | 20 | Gunner M.N. | Jan 1942 | Cobb, William L. | 26 | Leading Seaman | Nov 22 1942 |
| Beattie, Richard | 21 | Private | Sept 1943 | Cook, R.W. | 29 | Gunner | |
| Bellenie, Herbert Cecil | 20 | Gunner | Dec 11 1940 | Cook, Tommy | | M.N. | |
| Bland, Francis | 25 | Leading Steward | June 1941 | Cooper, James Purse | 16 | Officer Cadet | |
| Boardman, Richard | 36 | Acting Ldg Seaman | Sept 1942 | Cooper, N.M. | 29 | L/Cpl | |
| | | | | Curtis, John Thomas | 47 | M.N. | May 5 1942 |
| Boylen/Moore, Arthur | | | | | | | |
| Brannagan, John S | 27 | L/Corpl | May 31 1942 | Dalby, Douglas Haig | | M.N. | |
| Brignall, Edward John | | 4th Mate M.N. | | Davis, Fred | 23 | Flight Sergt. | June 1945 |
| Brown, Arthur S | 36 | | | Davis, John Thomas | 27 | Private | March 1943 |
| Brown, John James (Jimmy) | 23 | Private | Nov 20 1941 | Dodds, J.A.B. | 34 | M.N. | |
| Bulmer, M | 29 | Corporal | | Donachie, Robert | | Engineer M.N | Feb 1943 |
| Butler, J A | 24 | Gunner | June 16 1945 | Donaldson J.H. (Harry) | 31 | | May 1940 |
| | | | | Dunn, John Chapman | 27 | Gunner | April 6 1941 |
| Campion, James | 25 | | Feb 1943 | Dunn, Thomas | 27 | Private | Sept 1945 |

71

| Name | Age | Rank | Date of Death |
|---|---|---|---|
| Emmanuel, A | 27 | ex P.O. R.N. | Aug 24 1943 |
| Evans, Thomas Elliot | 30 | Gunner | June 1943 |
| Faith, Stewart T | 26 | M.N. | |
| Farrer, Edward | 18 | Ord Seaman R.N. | June 1944 |
| Farrer, John | | R.N. | |
| Ferguson | 21 | RAF | |
| Finnigan, William | 24 | Gunner | March 27 1945 |
| Flemming, Leslie Wallace | | Ord Seaman M.N. | |
| Forster, Fred | 36 | Sergt. | Dec 6 1944 |
| Foster, James Edward | 23 | Sergt. Air Gunner | Dec 1944 |
| Foster, William | 22 | Private | |
| Girdwood, J.E. | 21 | Sergeant | |
| Golightly, Arnold | | Flight Sergt. | Jan 1946 |
| Graham, Gordon | 25 | Trooper | April 1945 |
| Gray, John | 26 | Sapper | |
| Gregory, Frederick | 21 | M.N. | Aug 25 1940 |
| Gregory, Robert | 59 | M.N. | Aug 25 1940 |
| Griffiths, George Albert | 26 | Chief P. O. | April 13 1940 |
| Hall, John | | R.N. | |
| Hall, W. D. R. | 29 | Private | Mar 30 1944 |
| Henderson, Robert | 34 | L\Cpl | May 23 1940 |
| Hepple, Thomas Henry | 22 | | Nov 10 1942 |
| Hetherington, John P | 23 | Sergt Paratrooper | Dec 1942 |
| Higgins, Michael F S | 21 | R.N. | |
| Hogan, Edward Peter | 22 | Sergt. Air Gunne | |
| Howard, C L | | L\Bdr | |
| Hunter, Thomas | 24 | L\Cpl | Aug 1944 |
| Hurst, J.T. (Tommy) | 24 | Private | Jan 3 1941 |
| Inglis, George | 27 | M.N. | |
| Irving, Claude H | 33 | M.N. | |
| James, William | 32 | Gunner | Feb 13 1941 |
| Knight, Peter Herbert | 27 | | Feb 11 1944 |
| Lamb, Arthur H | | R.N. | May 1942 |
| Lanaway, Kenneth | 29 | Major | March 1944 |
| Langley, Harry Meadows | 22 | Stkr 1st Cl. R.N. | June 8 1940 |
| Laverick, H | 22 | A\B | |
| Ledger, Anthony | 20 | Sergt | Sept 1944 |
| Lennon, Henry H | 37 | LAC RAF VR | Dec 9 1943 |
| Lockwood, Joseph | | | Dec 1944 |
| Long, George Edward | 22 | L\Cpl | Sept 1944 |
| Loughlin | | | July 15 1941 |
| Loughlin, James M | 31 | Sergt | Oct 1944 |
| Lowther, George | 24 | Fusilier | March 1944 |
| McEvoy, PJ | 22 | | |
| McFarlane, Ninian Lyle | 23 | Sub Lieut. RNVR | May 1941 |
| McGough, Matthew | 24 | Private | March 30 1945 |
| McKenzie | | | |
| Maddison, Amos Rider | 20 | Sergt. Air Gunner | |
| Martin, Robert | 23 | Flying Officer | April 1945 |
| Maw, William | 20 | Ord. Seaman R.N. | |
| Miller, Arthur Herbert | 30 | 3rd Eng M.N. | Feb 15 1941 |
| Miller, Joseph M | 28 | | |
| Monaghan, James Joseph | 25 | Sapper | July 11 1941 |
| Muldoon,John | | | April 1943 |
| O'Connor, Harold Widdrington | | | Sergt. RAF |
| Oxlade, Charles | | | Aug 1941 |
| Parkinson, David William P | 21 | 4th Eng M.N. | July 7 1942 |
| Pattinson, George Ernest | | Private | Nov 3 1942 |
| Place, Leslie | 33 | Sergt RAC | Aug 1944 |
| Pollard, Norman (Military Medal) | | Private | |
| Potter, T | 21 | Gunner | |
| Price, Charles | 20 | M.N. | Aug 25 1940 |
| Pritchard, G. W. L. (Billy) | 24 | 4th Eng M.N. | Aug 1944 |
| Purvis, John George Michael | | M.N. | Jan 1943 |
| Pye, James Marsden | 21 | Sergt Flight Eng | Sept 1942 |
| Quin, William | | | Nov 1941 |
| Quinan, Edward (Curly) | | Acting A/B R.N. | Nov 27 1942 |
| Redman, Ritchard Douglas | 20 | Private | March 1945 |
| Richardson, Donald | | | |
| Richardson, Henry C | | Sergeant | July 4 1945 |
| Robertson, Wilfred | | | Dec 1943 |
| Robinson, J | 29 | Private | |
| Robinson, T | 21 | Private | |
| Robinson, Thomas Hayton | | Private | |
| Robinson, Thomas William | 28 | Flight Sergt RAF | Nov 1942 |
| Robson, E A (Alfred) | 28 | Trooper | |
| Rosebury, Frederick | 27 | | Aug 1943 |
| Sayers, Thomas | 21 | Private | Nov 6 1945 |
| Scott, William Henry | 19 | A/B M.N. | Feb 1941 |
| Skelton, Ronnie | 19 | RAF | |
| Smith, Joseph | 27 | Gunner | |
| Smith, Thomas | 21 | | May 24 1942 |
| Smith, William Henry | 33 | Corporal | Feb 1941 |
| Stanley, John | 21 | Able Seaman | Aug 28 1940 |
| Steel, John William | 29 | | April 1944 |
| Tansey, M | 21 | | |
| Tansey, Roger | 29 | M.N. | Aug 25 1940 |
| Tate, William | 21 | Stoker 1st Class | Oct 27 1939 |
| Taylor, Ronald | 23 | Sergt Air Gunner | Jan 1943 |
| Thirkell, Norman Cecil | 23 | Telegraphist R.N. | Aug 1941 |
| Thompson, Albert | 21 | | Dec 1944 |
| Thompson, George Thomas | 32 | Lance Corporal | April 1945 |
| Todd, Joseph (better known as Joe Tighe) | 26 | Lead. Sea. R.N. | Sept 26 1942 |
| Tonkinson, Sidney | | | |
| Vierow, Edward | 21 | F\O | August 1944 |
| Vincent, Arthur | 30 | Sergt | Oct 18 1939 |
| Waites, David | 19 | | Nov 1944 |
| Walton, R | 20 | Ordinary Seaman | |
| Ward, Arnold | 29 | | |
| Ward, George | | Gunner | |
| Warne, Norman | 18 | Signalman | June 3 1941 |
| | | Ordinary R.N. | |
| Watson, T P | 24 | Corporal | |
| Waugh, Ralph | | 3rd Officer M.N. | |
| Westbrook, George | 32 | Guardsman | May 1943 |
| Weston, James | 28 | | July 10 1944 |
| Williams, Joseph J | 27 | Ordinary Seaman | June 1944 |
| Williamson, Harry | 23 | Leading Stoker R.N. | |
| Willis, William | 26 | | Aug 1941 |
| Willis, | 32 | Gunner | |
| Wind, George | | Private | |
| Wood, William | 28 | | Oct 23 1941 |
| Wrathmall, J T | 21 | M.N. | |
| Young, Frederick Lee | | | June 8 1940 |

# Suddick Roots and Childhood Memories

John Gibson was born in the 1770s. He was a keelman on the river Tyne and he married Mary. They had at least eight children and lived on the crowded riverside at South Shields, off the busy East Holborn thoroughfare, within a few minutes walk of St Hilda's Parish Church. According to the book *Folk of South Shields* the Gibsons originated from the border country. In 1803 John and Mary's third child, William, was born. William was my great, great, great grandfather and he became a bottlemaker. He married Barbara Shadforth but in the 1830s tragedy struck the family when William and Barbara died in their 30s. Their orphaned son Robert is recorded in the 1841 census as a 12 year old apprentice living at Warn Court with a bottlemaker and his family called Cowans. Robert too became a bottlemaker at South Shields Bottleworks and he married Mary Bell of Hull. Early in 1851 they lived together at Warn Court, South Shields.

Henry Scott's Southwick Bottleworks on the riverside was expanding at that time. Bottlemakers were needed and many were lured from South Shields by the attraction of free accommodation at Low Southwick and free coals. 22 year old Robert Gibson and his young, pregnant wife settled in Southwick in 1851. Their first born John, my great, grandfather, was baptised in Holy Trinity Church at Southwick in February 1852 and I found a long line of my family in the parish registers. It was fascinating to view the original parish records to see where my ancestors, who were unable to write, had made their mark.

Robert and Mary had eight children. In 1871 they lived at 26 Victoria Street, a tenement building, where 29 persons lived.

John Gibson followed his grandfather and father into the bottlemaking industry. He married Elizabeth Lister of Sunderland. She is remembered as an old woman who wore a cap and smoked a pipe. There were grim times in the 1880s and 1890s. There had been a rapid population increase in Southwick; recessions of trade; poverty and disease; and a high infant mortality rate. Jack and Lizzie Gibson lost several children, but Adam (b.1883), my grandfather, and Mary survived. Mary later became Mary McGough and was said to have been a beautiful woman. Her portrait was painted by a local artist.

Adam Gibson married Mary Branney of Shotton - a Roman Catholic - and Adam will have promised to bring up the children in the Faith. Up until this period the Gibson family had been Church of England. Their youngest child was Jimmy Gibson (b.1920), my father. He served his apprenticeship as a riveter. "You had to be a man to be a riveter", and Jim had a reputation as a hard grafter. He was proud to go to work in the shipyards and rarely lost any time. For many men, boozing was an escape from their harsh industrial life and it seemed that Jim wasn't happy unless he had a pint in his hand. For a small man they reckon he could sup some ale, and he was a character. At pay-day on Fridays he became, like many of his peers, a weekend millionaire. After a few pints in Hogan's his face would glow with happiness. When he returned home after a good session and 'well oiled' it was as if someone had charged

him up. When he died in 1972 Southwick cemetery was crowded with friends he had made after a lifetime of living in Southwick and working in Wearside shipyards. A joke was cracked that all he left behind was an empty wallet and a broken pocket watch!

Jim had married Esther Meechin, a colliery lass from Wheatley Hill. It was a 'mixed marriage' and she too promised to bring up their children as Catholics. One hundred years after my ancestor had made a decision to move to Southwick I was born in hospital in 1951. I was taken to my grandmother's home at 61 Shakespeare Street, which is situated between Cobham Square and Barrie Square. It was there where I spent my childhood, and these are my memories as seen through my eyes as a young lad.

*Peter J. Gibson, Spring 1996*

I grew up with a group of lads who were born between 1949 and 1953. In our little world the late 1950s and early 1960s brought us a growing awareness of life in Southwick as well as some of the influences to which we were exposed. Our childhood wasn't unusual or out of the ordinary. Lads from neighbouring streets and squares will have had similar experiences. But it was unique because it was the only one we had and there was nothing to compare it with. Moreover, over a short period of time so much has changed and there are so many more dangers, influences and peer pressures put on today's young people in our rapidly changing society.

Southwick and the surrounding area was an interesting

Pal Palmer ©

# Barrie Square

and adventurous place for lads growing up in the late 1950s and early 1960s. Cobham Square and Barrie Square were typical playgrounds, the residents of Barrie Square tended to be more tolerant of noisy lads' games. It was there on the concrete that basic football and cricket skills were learnt. A burst plastic ball was fought over in a game of '10s half-time and 20s the winner', or 'gates', or 'three pots in' when the number of players were restricted.

Sometimes games were held up by the horses and carts of the ice cream man, or Maw's fruit

and veg, or Mr Whippey or Fella's ice cream vans. A fall of snow made a better game of it and provided a soft landing. My younger brother insisted on playing in his duffelcoat while the rest of us used our coats for goalposts. His running nose caused his sleeves to shine and glitter from elbow to cuff in the light of the lamp.

Kingie was a popular game when older lads aimed for bare legs with a worn tennis ball which whistled through the air at lightning speed before the stinging impact caused tears to the stunned victim. Queenie was a less hazardous game

but it was for girls and sissies. So too was hitchy bay (hopscotch) and skips. A game of alleys (marbles) created keen competition for beauties. Players owned a well used chipped favourite 'ponker' or shooter to play games like 'ponks', 'killer' and 'ringie'. Chuckstones and yo-yos came and went in phases.

Despite the high pitched noise of children at play during the warm summer evenings there was an anticipation and awareness of the dark nights drawing in, when another season heralded different games and interests. Tip and run and, of course, football were still

# Early 1960s

possible in the square under the lamp. Kick-the-tin, however, was more exciting when Stokoe shinned the lamp-post to slacken the bulb and put the square in darkness.

Whenever possible, staying in the house was avoided for fear of losing valuable playing time. Rainy periods were passed by reading the Beano and the Topper, the Dandy and the Beezer, or the Valiant and the Victor. Second hand action comics were bought from The Joke Shop along Southwick Road, which included Superman, Batman, Justice League of America, Wonder Woman, and Flash.

Although meal times were a hindrance there was always the wireless broadcasting entertainment spots such as The Jimmy Clitheroe Show; Workers' Playtime; as well as Uncle Mac's Children's favourites on Saturday mornings which seemed to play the same records each week, namely, The Runaway Train, Sparky who lost his echo, or was it stolen? Three Billy Goats Gruff and Tommy Steel - The Little White Bull. On Sundays the noise of Billy Cotton's Band Show - "Wakey, Wakey" - filled the room while families sat at the table for the traditional Sunday dinner. Foreign coins, which fit the gas meter, were kept handy in case the gas ran out in the middle of cooking, and a sixpence or shilling was not available. The coins were particularly needed on Thursdays - a bad day before the eagerly awaited pay day.

On the pop scene was Lonnie Donegan and that song about Tom Dooley; Frankie Vaughan - The Tower of Strength; and of course

Elvis and Rock n' Roll. Who can forget the teddy boys and their D.A.'s, drapes and drainpipes, winkle pickers and wedgies. They all carried combs and there was fascination at watching them pull out a quiff to form a roll of hair which rested above their brow. Chubby Checker and The Twist made an impression and then came The Beatles and others who revolutionised popular music, hairstyles and fashion.

The violence between rival teddy boy gangs called 'the red coats' and 'the blue coats' was replaced by the Mods and the Rockers who fought at Seaburn and Roker in the early 1960s.

By about 1958-60 most local families had obtained their first television sets. Many rented a 17 inch black and white model from Rediffusion. It probably helped to cause the decline of 'the Pictures' ('the Flicks') but the children's matinee on Saturday at the Marina at Fulwell was still popular after the closure of the Savoy in 1959. Popular programmes on those early tellies included Terry O' Neill and of course George Romaine on the One O' Clock Show; Wagon Train; Cheyenne; as well as Arthur Haynes, the tramp comedian and Charlie Drake. On Saturday afternoons wrestlers entertained us. Comedians like Jackie Palloe and Mick McManus bashed up opponents while the wardance of Billy Two Rivers frightened off others. Pinfalls, submissions, suplex, forearm smash, backbreaker and Dad practising holds on us and forcing us to submit.

Between Barrie Square and Cobham Square there was vacant waste land known as 'The Sparies' ('the field')          on the 1965 aerial view on page 83 . Access was possible through a cut from Cobham Square or from a back garden. A rough path led to a bare patch of ground, near to the football ground fence, where local derbies, cup finals and test matches took place. But woe betide the one who did not 'field his innings'. The Sparies and the square soon became inadequate for the needs of growing lads and more competitive games took place on Thompson Park. A corner of Wearmouth football ground was used too, but a pre-planned escape route was organised in the event of a  groundsman's appearance.

In a corner of the Sparies near to old Mr Burnett's enclosed allotment a group of older lads, which we called the Clarkies, from

**Clarkies Den**

Cobham Square, were spotted disappearing into a hole in the ground which was covered by a sort of trap-door. Curious about what was going on we entered the hole while one remained outside to keep watch. The mystery of how the earth was held up was solved and we marvelled at the feat of engineering by our enemies. A large hole had been dug and planks of timber were placed across it.

Old mats and carpets were laid over the planks and soil shovelled over and levelled. Or there may have been old doors keeping the soil up. It was a den or gang hut and we were envious. The visit was cut short by word that the Clarkies were coming. We couldn't let them catch us because tortures included placing a large stone or lump of concrete on the victims body and standing on it while the victim squealed beneath the weight. A hurried exit was made and we did a bunk into the football ground, followed by shouted warnings from the Clarkies. The Clarkies were a quick witted, humorous lot but the Barrie Square gang did not wait to find out whether they were kidding. On one occasion Giggey Clark threw some very young boys into the hole and stood on the trapdoor wickedly laughing while frantic cries were heard beneath him from boys afraid of the blackness. They were allowed to emerge after a few minutes, visibly shaken by their ordeal while we shouted insults from the safety of Langley's back garden.

We attempted to make a

similar underground den but the failure was made worse by the crowd from Cobham Square that gathered at the top of the cut and gloated and jeered when the construction collapsed and was immediately abandoned. A fight broke out between one girl from each of the two rival squares which was broken up by parents. It seemed that everybody from Cobham Square was a Clarkie. Shortly afterwards their den on the Sparies was destroyed, but it was not known by whom!

Guy Fawkes night was an important event and the Sparies was the site of enormous bonfires. The Clarkies controlled the Sparies and our gang from Barrie Square delighted in sneaking onto it to light their bonfire under the cover of darkness. One by one the Clarkies left school and 'The Field' eventually became ours.

During the weeks leading up to November 5th excitement grew when any old material that burnt well was collected. Old car tyres and canvass were sought after, and old armchairs were scragged for coins.

In October 1959 a bonfire stacked against the fence in Hall's back garden at 63 Shakespeare Street caught fire and spread to the greenhouse of adjoining No 61 where we lived. The bedroom where I slept with my two brothers was filling with smoke as the strong wind fanned the flames which were threatening to engulf the houses. Mr Briggs and his son from across the street entered the house and rescued us. Mr Briggs' daughter Rosie telephoned for the Fire Brigade and they put out the fire. A Fire Brigade spokesman said, "There is a history in the area of bonfires on vacant ground being set alight by youths and this could have been the case here … This could have been a tragedy with a number of people losing their lives."

The bonfire on the field was conscientiously guarded and mud traps were made in the cut. At the risk of a good hiding raids were made on bonfires in nearby areas. There was a reluctance, however, to venture as far as Marley Pots. The Marley Potters from Marley Crescent and Maplewood Avenue were a tough lot and a different breed. They were known to hide in a hollow or den inside the stacked bonfire to give the illusion that it wasn't guarded. Unsuspecting raiders were surprised and beaten up, sometimes with studded army belts. On one occasion lasses fought off 'Prefabbers' from the Lichfield Road area who had raided the bonfire which stood at the top of the hill behind Maplewood Avenue.

One Marley Potter of that time who could hardly be forgotten was Archie X. He was known to rub lads faces in horse manure, and during a chase by a farmer, being older and stronger, he had the confidence to outrun the others. He would drop back behind younger Marley Potters who were in a frantic bid to escape, and snigger wickedly as he tripped the tailenders. On other occasions he forced lads to dig holes and caned them when they stopped before he said so. "Aye, he would tempt us to go over the quarries with Mars Bars and sweets, and on the way back he would kick the shit out of us!" - Billy P. Archie X was wicked to his own kind and there would be little sympathy for a strange laddo from the squares.

*Marley Potters in the early 1960s. Back row left to right: Philip McGarley, Alan Cowe, Eddie Davison. Front row: Eddie Wooton, Mickey Pemberton, Billy Pemberton, Stevie Brown.*

*The photograph was taken at the west end of Marley Pots playing fields. In the background across the top of the hill was the old quarry path. Either side of the path were allotments. Carley Hill housing estate now occupies the site. At the bottom of the hill on the right was Archie Donaldson's piggery. Billy Pemberton (pictured above) remembers: "When he caught us in the yard he would give us a clip and threaten to throw us in beside the big boar. On one occasion he hung me over the stye by the ankles and told me not to go into his yard gain."*

77

Another Marley Potter was Freddie X who spent much of his time in the quarries. He was up with the larks and went bird nesting and catching rabbits from dawn until dusk. "The character in the film 'Kes' didn't have a look in", is a recollection of Freddie X. Other activities included camping in the quarries, raiding nearby apple orchards, as well as pinching turnips and helping Archie X to set fire to haystacks. A favourite playground for young Marley Potters was the 'Tarzan Tree', and sometimes lads were 'caught short' in the countryside. Most would choose a discreet spot, but not Freddie. He preferred to use the Tarzan Tree and he didn't seem to care who saw his backside. Those playing beneath were often forced to fun for cover.

necessary to trespass on farmers' fields in search of rare eggs. Sometimes it was every lad for himself and younger brothers were considered a worrying burden and weren't allowed to go. There was a hierarchy in the gang and the best fighter was the leader, followed by a pecking order. I will have been about 9 or 10 years old at this time and it was generally accepted that older lads could fight younger ones. But it wasn't accepted that some older girls could fight younger boys. Girls were not allowed in the gang and gang members could not take the humiliation of being beaten by a girl. Consequently, tough girls like the one I'm afraid to mention were avoided!

There were two main routes to the quarries: The Marley Pots end, by-passing the allotments and

Place was usually a safe one because we knew some of the Carley Doggers, but I can remember getting into a fight on one occasion. At the top of Carley Hill Road, past the scrapyard and Moss' Farm on the

**Tough Girl**

left, and the 'Cricketey' over the high wall on the right, was an inclined walled path (which still exists today) which led to the 'Quarry Path'. Over the right wall of the inclined path was an overgrown quarry known as 'The Jungle', where there was a pumping station for the colliery, and a popular rope swing attached to a large tree. The gang was entering another world as swallows and swifts swooped down the pathway, and numerous crows circled above their nests on the cliff faces.

Along the quarry path was an extensive and deep Fulwell quarry known as 'The Binny' where the council tipped rubbish. It was a booming industry down there as men and boys salvaged scrap for a 'weigh in'. Football pitches occupy the site today.

To the left of the path was another old quarry where colliery waste was tipped. Coal was separated from slag by men and boys whose red lips and whites of eyes stood out from dust covered blackened faces. I was a regular

**The Tarzan Tree**

The search for birds' nests to steal their eggs encouraged lads to venture away from the small, safe world of the Sparies and the two squares. Confrontations with other gangs could occur and the threat of chases by older lads or farmers was ever present. It was

piggeries; and the Carley route which included a short cut nervously taken by trespassing across Wearmouth Colliery Welfare near to the tennis courts. A wary eye was kept for Norton, the groundsman, and his alsation. The progression through Carley visitor to this area to take cigarettes and water to my Dad who went for coal during slack periods in the shipyards in the early 1960s. I can remember the fascination of the buzz of activity when another eagerly awaited wagon arrived. A lad spotted a 'big roundy' ( a very large lump of coal) and as the load was rising on the hydraulics he clambered into the wagon to slide off with the roundy and claim it before others moved in to the new pile. It was common on the streets of Southwick to see men and lads struggling to balance bags of coal on an old bike. 'Coal yacker' was a derogatory term used for people who went for coal in the quarries, but many families relied on the tipping for their heating. Despite the quality of life improving compared to the 1920s and 1930s life in the early 1960s could still be a struggle sometimes, and all of the time for some families.

When tipping ceased and the surface coal was taken away, coal could be extracted by digging beneath the surface, but it was hard graft. Jackie Hargreaves, who lived on the corner of Shakespeare Street and Cobham Square, was a well known character and despite his small stature had a reputation for hard work. He was a professional and 'the salt of the earth'. He would load up his boneshaker 'Dynamite' with four bags of coal and freewheel down the inclined path toward Carley Place. "Out the way!", he would shout as Dynamite gathered speed and lads scattered in all directions. He seemed oblivious to the possibility of colliding with traffic which came from the direction of Carley Lodge.

The old quarries supplied the fuel for roaring fires in big old fire-places which greeted children on cold mornings. Bedrooms were like ice-boxes before the days of central heating and little cold feet were warmed by stone ginger beer bottles filled with boiling water. A hot oven shelf wrapped in an old sheet was another method of warming beds because conventional hot water bottles were a luxury in those days.

"Out The Way"

In the old Fulwell quarries were the remains of buildings and sheds known as 'The Ghost Town'. It was an adventure playground ready to explore, but the buildings and the deep disused kilns were an unwitting danger. On the embankment above The Ghost Town were the targets for a firing range. Further on into the country was Spuggies Arch and Boldon Pond with all of its wildlife.

Another favourite birdnesting spot was along the riverbank at 'The Boaty' and further on near the concrete boat and Hylton Colliery was "The Red Wood". Slagheaps towered above and encroached on the wood. In retrospect another unwitting danger before the tragedy of Aberfan. The Boaty could be approached by a large disused embankment which had been constructed to carry the railway from Hylton over the Queen Alexandra Bridge.

Access to the embankment was by scaling a wall of large red blocks in Clockwell Street. The top of the embankment was a high vantage point which looked down into a noisy, busy shipyard. The Boaty was in sight and progress along the embankment caused an air of anticipation in youngsters eager to pillage birds' nests.

With hindsight, stealing eggs from birds was a repugnant activity, but all lads went birdnesting at that time. There was pride to show off a good collection of eggs. We had our rules though: we did not take eggs from blackbirds, thrushes, sparrows and linnets because they were common. We did not 'scarp' nests (take all of the eggs from a nest) unless, of course, we located rare eggs and all of the gang wanted one. We did not 'tuggy' nests (destroy them), though some did who had been there before us. And we did not take 'dippy' eggs which were ready to hatch. There was nothing better than to find a nest full of young 'uns, but we had to be careful when returning to see their development in case the mother deserted.

The Boaty also provokes memories of a fox cub which was captured there, but was taken from the Barric Square lads by Marley Potters on the old railway embankment.

Marley Potters had a bad enough reputation but stories told around fires on The Sparies made the gang aware that Castletowners could be much worse. They were said to tie lads to trees and force 'spelks' (wood splinters) under their fingernails! Despite the fear of

Photograph by Ian S. Carr

*J 270-6-0 65788 passes Austin & Pickersgill's shipyard and heads towards Monkwearmouth in 1963. On the right is the old railway embankment which led from Queen Alexandra Bridge to Castletown junction. The embankment provided access to the 'Boaty'. The sloping wall on the right exists today near the footbridge leading from the bottom of Burntland Avenue over Wessington Way.*

Castletowners and Marley Potters another danger lurked in the quiet countryside for lads who had strayed from the safety of the squares. We had long outgrown being afraid of 'Dickie Darkie' and 'Jack Frost', but 'Sandshoe Sammy' could do terrible things to children. Sandshoe Sammy, who was the bogeyman, and may well have changed his shoes to avoid being recognised. All lone men were treated with suspicion and given a 'wide berth'. Despite The Boaty having a notorious reputation for attracting dubious characters the gang felt safety in numbers.

We knew what could happen to children and the dangers were reinforced in an incident in a back lane near Roker Park football ground and next to the bus depot. Panels were missing in the fence next to a bus shed and there were paintings in antique frames between the gap of the fence and the shed. Two or three paintings were pulled out and at least one was dropped and the glass broken on the cobble stones. A man opened a back door to see what was happening. The gang ran to the top of the back lane and I was left to clear the broken glass. One painting wasn't damaged - The Laughing Cavalier - it was the original too, or so we thought! While I was busy I noticed the man disappearing into his backyard and returning at intervals to the back door. When the mess was cleared I made my way towards my mates who were waiting at the top of the back lane - and I'm glad they were there. The Laughing Cavalier was almost as big as I was, as I approached level with the doorway the man grinned and pulled his undone trousers apart - "That's a better picture son, isn't it?" he said. Heart pounding with shock and my head almost bursting with fear I thought he would grab me as I ran desperately to my mates, and still clutching the master. By the time I reached the top of the back lane the group were doubled up with laughter at my ashen face and distressed expression. They must have known about that man but they denied it. The experience left me with a great empathy for children subjected to sexual abuse.

There were many other activities and pastimes and it was difficult to become bored. Writing down car registration numbers from the Savoy steps in about 1960 now seems a bit of a joke in comparison with today's vehicle crowded green. We searched for conkers in the grounds of Hylton Castle or explored the old air raid shelter on the Bunny Hill. Newcastle Road Baths provided a good venue for some lads who liked to show off on the springboard. Wednesday nights, Friday nights and Saturday mornings were popular sessions. We were allowed in for one hour but there was no timing system. Occasionally a locker boy would emerge from the locker rooms to make a hand inspection. Those with shrivelled fingers caused by long exposure in the water were ordered out. Sometimes Bob would do the inspection. Bob was a heavily built and humorous character who often wore a boilersuit and wellies turned over at the top. He would quickly inspect the fingers of crowds of lads who were standing at the sides of the baths, and were either resting, talking or weighing up the talent. Diversions were made to avoid him and the one hour session was stretched to one and a half or sometimes two hours. I can remember on many occasions coming out of the baths starving and with a headache after making sure that I had had "my moneys worth". A cup of hot oxo and a cracker from the baths shop was a welcomed warm-up from the coldish water and draughty changing rooms.

*Newcastle Road Baths celebrated its 60th birthday in June 1996. When the baths opened in 1936 the Corporation redeemed a promise made to the people of Southwick in 1928. The provision of a swimming baths in the vicinity of Southwick was one of the conditions of Southwick joining Sunderland. The facility has been well used by generations of Suddickers, and it is endearingly remembered as the place where many learnt to swim.*

Alternatively, there was the Police Boys Club in the 'Whitehouse' on The Green which had been vacated by Southwick Social Club, and where we competed for an attractive silver cup at three-a-side football.

Southwick Social Club sports day was the highlight of the summer holidays when prizes and silver cups were keenly competed for in races. The packed buses, hired by the Club, took families to Seaburn Camp for a memorable and well organised event.

A day out at Seaburn was within easy reach of youngsters. It was three-half-pence bus fare on the No 18 but many buses were full before they arrived at Southwick during the summer months. Waiting at the Morgan Street bus stop could be entertaining by watching the two monkeys climbing up and down a high pole in the garden of the corner house in Ridley Street. The strong smell of sea air and seaweed greeted us at the terminus and there was a donkey ride on the beach, the miniature railway, the boating lake, candy floss, toffee apples, Notrianni's ice-cream and, of course, chips and Seaburn sandwiches (egg and tomato). The fair was set back in those days and backing on to a golf course. There are memories of The Big Dipper, The Ghost Train, What the Butler Saw, the Win a Woodbine machine. We couldn't afford to do it all, in fact we couldn't afford to do much of it and there was the temptation to spend the bus fare and walk home. A weary trek for tired young legs.

Mr Helmsley led organised games on Thompson Park during the early 1960s and they were well patronised. Boxing, golf, stilts, hockey, basketball, rounders and football equipment and other items were borrowed from the hut next to the swingey park. Mr Medcalf was the parkie and I can remember many kids falling off the Monkey Climber and being treated by him. The park was packed during the annual six week summer holidays and old Mr Medcalf had a busy time of it.

*Bob Medcalf was 'parkie' at Thompson Park for over thirty years. "He was everybody's grandad", recalls his grandaughter Annette. Bob had worked for the Thompson sisters who lived in a large house where the council compound is situated today. When Margaret Thompson left the estate to the people of Sunderland to make into a park, provision was made for their employees to be taken on by the Council. Mr Medcalf was employed as parkie for life and generations of Southwick children played in the park in his care. He retired in 1969 and died in 1984 aged 80.*

## A Boxing Lesson

A boxing ring was erected as part of the organised games on Thompson Park. Large boxing gloves were supplied which seemed to weigh a ton. I'd had a couple of victories with what I thought was a unique boxing style - Going in with my head down and bowling in punches like a windmill had seen off my opponents within seconds. However, on one beautiful summer day I took on a mate from school. Another mate acted as my second and asked me if I could scrap him. "Why-aye," I replied unconvincingly. My second gave me advice and coaching, and I opened up in typical style in front of a largish crowd. However, my opponent stepped back and selected punches thudded into the top of my head. Round two followed a similar pattern and I spent more time on the ground spitting out grass. By the end of round two I was getting such a pasting that my second had deserted the corner. I hadn't been this far before and in round three I was feeling exhausted. I was hoping the referee would stop the fight seeing that my second wasn't there to throw in the towel. A man watching the fight told me to keep my head up. As an eleven year old I couldn't see the logic in this advice. It meant that I would be getting hit in the face instead of on top of the head. After the fight my opponent and I walked for a welcome drink from the ornate fountain which had metal cups attached to chains which stood next to the swingy park. I was choked at the defeat and I decided to retire from the ring to concentrate on football!

*Thompson Park in August 1967.*

The Methodists ran the Boys Brigade which took place in the Sunday School building situated on the corner of Dean Terrace and Mary Street. There was a military tone to it and the officer in charge was helped by what appeared to be two junior officers or sergeants who had probably progressed from the ranks. Activities included trampolining which was good fun. With hindsight people were giving up their time to organise events and activities for any Southwick lad interested in joining the Brigade irrespective of their religion. But, unfortunately, boys will be boys. At a certain time of the evening we were ordered to line up for an inspection. The officer would march out of his office, and a sergeant would give the order - "Atten—shun!" There was silence as we stood at attention in our best street clothes, which must have been a bit rough, although some of the regulars wore uniforms. It was too much for some of us to handle as the officer, wearing his side cap and swagger stick tucked under his armpit, looked each of us up and down. It was a strange situation to be in for lads new to the Brigade and some of us fought hard not to laugh. Ronnie Langley would be the first to break down followed by Stokoe. It was infectious and uproariously funny as we fought to control ourselves. The officer and his two assistants kept straight faces and carried on with the inspection before returning to the office.

On another occasion prayers were said and I told a junior officer that my two brothers and I could not join in with the prayers because we were Roman Catholics. We were taken in to see the officer in charge who asked me why we could not pray. I quoted from the Catechism in my reply that we could not take part in the services or prayers of a false religion. It was also something which had been reinforced to us at school. The officer retorted calmly that if we could not join in with the prayers we could not attend the Boys Brigade. I did not expect that ultimatum but it was fair enough. It did not take me long to weigh it up. There was nothing organised for the youth of our church and, besides, we were having a good time at the Boys Brigade. So we joined in with the prayers! My service in the Boys Brigade did not last very long but one of my younger brothers was a member for several years.

*1965 aerial view of the Squares area of Southwick. Shakespeare Street (on the left) heads northwards. The ABC squares branch off to the right. Barrie Square and Cobham Square are second and third, respectively, from bottom of photograph. The 'Sparies' can be seen between the two squares. Hahnemann Court is being built (bottom right), and Carley Hill Road, to the right of the building site, leads to Carley Hill Farm and the quarries.*

## The Queenies

Two elderly spinster sisters lived across the road from Beaumont Street shops. They were strange characters who we knew as 'The Queenies'. The short, fat one appeared to dominate the dark, thin one. You could scrape the muck off both of them and I can remember being afraid of them when I was very young. Older children told us they were witches whose overgrown back garden, which backed onto the 'Pigeon Field' before Cato Square was built, was infested with snakes. They often fought and argued with each other. On one occasion when we were going to school the dominant one struck her sister over the head with a poker and she bled profusely. The fat one stood on the front doorstep wielding the poker, her tongue darting in and out like a lizard as she denied her sister entry to the house. I cannot remember ever hearing either sister speak - just grunts and squeals.

*The annual Pancake Race in Cato Street on 'Pancake Tuesday' 1958. The race was organised from Holy Trinity Church Hall in Cato Street.*

*Players and supporters from Southwick Social Club and Southwick pubs are pictured before the annual charity Boxing Day push-ball match in 1956 at Wearmouth Colliery Welfare Football Ground. The players competed in a game of football and pushball, each half lasted for twenty minutes in both matches. The challenge matches took place from about 1956 to about 1960. The pushball can be seen behind the group.*

*Wearmouth Colliery Welfare was the venue of semi-finals and finals at the beginning of the light nights. It was the usual entry - ower the wall to avoid paying, and to join large crowds being entertained by highly competitive cup ties like Maplewood Star verses Timpsonians. Wearmouth played on Saturday afternoon and it was another excuse to enter the ground to play headers between the touchline and barriers. The team was loyally supported by two*

*handicapped brothers - a quiet one and Andre, who loudly and enthusiastically shouted them on. He kept the score on paper and made other spectators aware of the current situation. Dennis McGregor was another character who updated spectators at Wearmouth with Sunderland's progress, which was received on transistor radios. It was sad when Southwick's Wembley was sold to build Coldstream Avenue but the ground had suffered much from vandalism.*

Most lads kept football scrapbooks. Right are the autographs from a season when Sunderland were heading for promotion to the old First Division, until they were unexpectedly beaten one-nil by Chelsea at Roker Park in the last game of the season.

Surely no other period in living memory can compare to the atmosphere and passion which was generated at Roker Park during the early 1960s. Teams were said to be afraid to come to Roker Park and were intimidated by the famous Roker Roar before the days of chanting crowds. The average home gate in 1962-63 season was 40,000. In the early '60s there were the memorable F.A. cup-ties against Tottenham, Man Utd. and Everton; and of course the promotion season of 1963-64.

The players were heroes to lads at an impressionable age: King Charlie Hurley with his heading ability; George Herd's ball skills; hardmen Jimmy McNab and Len Ashurst; the reflexes of Monty; as well as the class of Stan Anderson and free scoring Brian Clough. It was shocking for us lads when he received a serious knee injury on Boxing Day 1962 which virtually ended his career.

The two shillings entry (10p) into the Fulwell End, before the roof was erected over the terraces, was sometimes further than our pocket money would stretch. We would wait for an opportunity to climb over the 'Clicky', which was a one way revolving gate providing an exit from the Fulwell End. The Clicky was made up of a series of metal bars which acted as a ladder to a narrow gap at the top where small bodies could crawl through.

SUNDERLAND ASSOCIATION FOOTBALL CLUB LTD.

PLAYERS' AUTOGRAPHS.     SEASON 1962-63.

Goalkeeper Jimmy Montgomery was a 'Suddick' lad who lived with his parents at the north corner of Lichfield Road and Old Mill Road. He would always oblige young'uns who called at the house for his autograph.

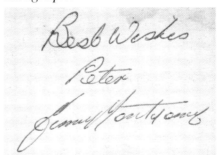

There was conflict between life on the streets and the standards and expectations preached from the pulpit and at school. School discipline was strict and it was sometimes wise to conform to the demands made on Catholic youngsters. I started school in 1956 and in the early years it was the practice to salute nuns and teachers when filing past them on mornings or when approaching them for some reason.

The Catechism was taught in crowded classrooms e.g. St Hilda's J2B contained 50 pupils in 1960. We were required to learn the answers to the questions off by heart:- Who made you? Why did God make you? As we got older the answers became longer and more difficult. It was the cane for not knowing the Catechism.

Novena on Thursday evenings was followed by Confession. There was a large queue to confess to a popular priest compared to the confessional box of an Irish priest who was difficult to understand and admonished us for our transgressions. Teachers who supervised the event shuttled unlucky pupils from one queue to the other. It was a mistake to arrange to meet 'non-Catholic' friends outside of church. Playing with fellow good catholic children was strongly recommended. And, besides, we were taught that Protestants would not be saved on Judgement Day because they did not follow the one true religion. It would have been a lonely life relying on Catholic friends. Some best mates went to High Southwick School.

The depth of religious influence depended on the teacher. There was an emphasis on the importance of Baptism to remove original sin committed by Adam. Babies who died before they were christened would go to a place called Limbo and would not see God. Seven was said to be the age of reasoning when we could commit sin. Those who died in a state of venial sin would go to Purgatory to suffer for their sins before they entered Heaven. But there was the real fear of suffering for eternity in the fires of Hell by dying in a state of mortal sin - the penalty for more serious offences and for missing Mass on Sunday. Attending Mass on the first Friday of every month for nine months, however, ensured a peaceful death. The indoctrination continued with the insensitive teaching that the end of the world would probably come soon by fire and brimstone and not by water as in the Great Flood. We believed everything they told us and as an eight year old I had frightening nightmares which depicted the end of the world.

I was eight years old when I was Confirmed by the Bishop of Hexham and Newcastle. It was a big event at St Hilda's. We each chose a Confirmation name taken from a saint. At that young age I was intrigued about the story of St Christopher, the patron saint of travellers, who had carried the infant Jesus across a river or stream. During the crossing the infant became heavier and heavier to test

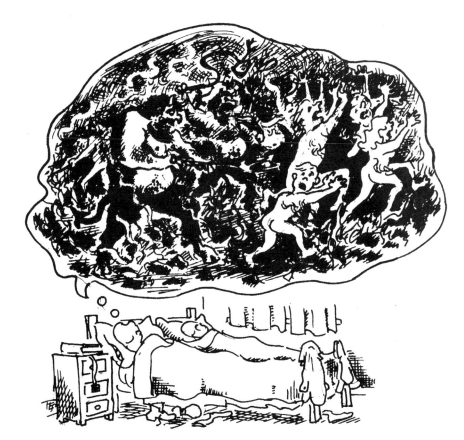

**Nightmare**

St Christopher. Consequently, Christopher became part of my name and as we were encouraged to pray to the saints he became my favourite. It appeared that I had been wasting my time because several years later the Catholic Church decided that St Christopher hadn't existed and the incident with the infant Jesus hadn't happened.

The Latin Mass lasted for about forty-five minutes. It was a long time for a youngster and day dreaming helped to pass away the time. We had to be free from mortal sin and fast for three hours before taking communion. I can remember several people fainting during the Mass. The fast was later reduced to one hour.

Taking Communion could be embarrassing when kneeling at the altar revealed worn shoes. Even Tuf shoes wore out and we had to wait for the next Provident club to come round. After Communion we

**Holy Communion and Holy Soles**

waited eagerly for the words: "ITE MISSA EST" (Go, the Mass is ended). And we were back on the streets and fields again kicking lumps out of each other at football.

There was an alternative to Mass, however, when sometimes the two pennies originally intended for the two collections were spent on four half-penny milk chews; which I sucked during a walk to Hylton Castle; or to the Wheatsheaf in the drizzle; or in the bus shelter on The Green, and the demolition site of the old Manor House. The answer to the anticipated question was usually found in the playground on Monday mornings: "Who said Mass?" Some teachers were a step ahead of street-wise kids and: "What was the sermon about?" or "What colours did the priest wear?" Were questions which stumped non-attenders. There were advantages of being a Catholic though - a holiday on St Patrick's Day, the patron saint of Ireland, as well as receiving some Shamrock at Mass to pin to a coat.

There was respect for and a certain amount of fear of priests. Some members of families who were not practising the religion crowded into the bathroom or greenhouse rather than face the priest who had paid a visit to the home during his rounds.

The education had seemed to improve at St Hilda's in smaller classes after English Martyrs Junior School had been opened in September 1960. Religion became more intense under the new regime at St Hilda's and it was obvious that efforts were being made to improve the image of the school. Pressure was put on families to send children to school in a uniform and there were casualties: "My da' was disabled and couldn't work regularly. There were six of us and my ma' couldn't afford one

uniform between all of us never mind one each! My ma' was often down to the school because of the hassle we were getting over the uniform. We eventually left the Catholic Schools to go to a state school where a uniform was not required. A burden was lifted from me and I was even picked for the football team." - D.C. And - "I had to wear wellies for school during the summer. Johnny, who lived a few doors from us, wore wellies for school as well, and that made me feel a little bit better" W.P.

We were taught about the persecution of Catholics throughout the centuries. I have often wondered if some teachers were aware that they may have been persecuting some of the children in their care! Later, attitudes mellowed and rules changed. There had to be changes, but thousands of us had gone through it. Generations born after the war questioned the superstitions, rituals and beliefs which had been passed down the centuries.

In September 1962 St Thomas Aquinas Boys School was opened. I was in the first intake, and although we didn't realise it at the time I and my fellow 11 plus failures were being directed towards manual occupations in industry.

'Batman' (or 'Legs') the headmaster was a strict disciplinarian. The cane was administered for almost anything. In the mornings when the whistle blew the various classes lined up behind the class prefect, or the best fighter. We filed into the school in military fashion and passed teachers who inspected the uniform. It was the cane for muddy shoes, for not wearing a school tie, for being late, for walking on the grass, for chewing, for forgetting homework or not delivering an absentee note and for any other misdemeanour. Being cheeky to teachers was a rarity and just wasn't done. A major breach of discipline like playing with light switches by turning them on and off was dealt with by 'six of the best'.

In the cloakroom beneath the coat hooks and near to the floor were small boxes where outdoor

---

### Chip Chop Quiz

Another name for the cane was 'the chop' and the last ten minutes of some Maths lessons at St Thomas Aquinas Boys School were taken up by 'Chip Chop Quiz'. The Quizmaster asked each pupil in turn a question which was usually from the tables (1 to 12) - "Seven nines?" "Er, er," replied Jimmy, as he played for time in an effort to come up with the answer. "Come on boy! Seven nines?" A wrong answer accumulated one cane. The quiz was particularly hilarious in a 'B' stream where mental arithmetic was a weakness. There were mass canings as the queue for punishment extended from the front of the class to well into the aisles. The chop could either be taken on the hand or over the backside, which caused a sickly feeling. But there could be a last minute reprieve. "Double or quits?" asked the teacher cynically. The choice was to either take one cane owed or request another question. Another wrong answer, however, meant two canes, or double or quits again. The game carried on to the amusement of the class who had answered correctly at the first attempt. The teacher was a rugby player and a well built man. He didn't lay it on in Chip Chop Quiz but he was capable of doing so for something more serious!

**Batman**

shoes were exchanged for plimsolls. Wellies had to be folded to fit into the box but they could spring out. Older lads were known to run through the aisles and pull out shoes and boots here and there. It was a horror for me as an eleven year old to find a shoe or welly was missing at the end of the day. The procedure was to report the matter to 'Batman', and several of us made our way reluctantly through the canteen to his office. We were invited in to choose our footwear from the collection he had picked up from the cloakroom floor throughout the day. Excuses were not accepted as he produced his 'cane' - a monster which appeared to be a sawn off snooker cue with tape around it. I can still remember the butterflies in the pit of my stomach at the sight of it. Most of us learned to take the punishment with dignity and pride, particularly when it was carried out in front of

the class. There was no flinching and it was hoped the teacher would make a good strike and not cause injury to finger tips, thumbs or wrists. Certain teachers laid it on and we learned to hold out our hands as high as possible to reduce the leverage. The cane produced a painful stinging red weal which throbbed for ages afterwards. Batman's stick, however, was different and much worse - a painful dull thud which felt like the stick had penetrated to the rear of the hand.

There were those, of course, who weren't bothered by the cane but those who were smart knew their place, conformed wherever possible and tried to avoid corporal punishment.

Most of us couldn't wait to leave school and that day soon arrived. Life for us changed quickly and drastically when we joined the adult world of employment at the

age of 15. We had to grow up fast in the rough environment of industry where there were jobs and apprenticeships for all 1966 school leavers. Some teachers had created a lasting impression, however; like Miss Quesnel and Mr Flynn for their kindness at St Hilda's Juniors; and Mr Scales (Maths) and Mr Naisby (English) who were strict, good teachers and earned respect at St Thomas Aquinas Boys School.

# Southwick Shipyard's Last Days

A rare view of the shipyard from the tower of Holy Trinity Church in 1981.

Left – The main gate in the mid 1980s.

Right – The last launch at Southwick and on the Wear was the *Superflex November* ferry on December 12th 1988. The event was in sharp contrast to the success of a little over a decade previously. In 1977 A&P won The Queen's Award for Industry for export achievement.

After the Southwick Shipyard of North East Shipbuilders Ltd (better known as 'Pickies') controversially closed in 1988 the *Sunderland Echo* reported of the auction of plant and equipment in November 1990: " … Which many Wearsiders view with amazement. They still cannot believe that assets at the yard, described as the finest in Europe, are being sold off as a prelude to the arrival of the demolition crew which will level the buildings." The disposal of the yard's equipment forced home to Wearsiders the stark reality that the long fight to save the yard had finally ended.

The sadness surrounding the closure was a repeat in history in Southwick's history when Robert Thompson's shipyard closed in 1932. An *Echo* reporter wrote at the auction in June 1932: " … The last ships have slid proudly down the ways. All is silence and weed and rust … As I looked out of the window of the sale room through the forest of pitch poles and steel gantries I saw the ghosts of fine ships gliding down on the broad back of the river. I saw them ploughing evenly across the oceans of the earth, wherever trade routes are known, but they faded away … Everything sold pathetically cheap. Cranes were almost as cheap as nuts and bolts. Lot 46 described as a 12 foot steel jib crane went for a paltry 15 shillings (75p)."

The poignancy of the Pickies closure, however, meant that shipbuilding in Southwick ceased permanently after a history of over two centuries. Nevertheless, Pickies not only produced skilled men to build ships in harsh conditions, the yard (and others on the Wear) also manufactured characters – and by the boatload.

Apprentices were looked after by the men but they were often initiated into the ways of the yard.

Fifteen and sixteen-year-olds could be sent for a cap-full of nail holes, a long stand, a wire netting oil can or a bucket full of steam. And there was always the threat of greasing private parts with tallow used on the ways. It was a male only workplace and sometimes it could become hostile and aggressive.

Shipyard humour was subtle, but sometimes it could be cutting and cruel. Taking the 'mickey' seemed to get some men through the day. Some saw it as a challenge and a test of their intelligence to wind someone up and get him to 'bite'. Everyone and every angle was tapped for weaknesses. Unless, of course, he was a hard hitter like 'Jawbreaker' and then nobody said nowt to the likes of him or tried to wind him up. It was a mistake to take the bait and there was little sympathy or respect to someone who bit because others would join in to 'reel him in'. Care was taken about what was said and done so as to avoid being a target, and nicknames often stuck for life. There were some tough, hard natured men working in the yards and there was little compassion for physical flaws. But men like 'Bobby Bent Legs', 'Horse Head' and 'Bobby Nee Legs' didn't seem to mind their sobriquet. There were others of course: 'The Ginger Gissie' swilled down the beer; 'Mr Clean' was always spotless; 'The Walker Brothers' were noted for their yard rambles; and 'Scenty Gob' was well spoken. There was also 'Tommy Tomato' who brought homegrown tomatoes to work for the gaffer; 'Spider' who was a crawler; 'The Body' was always lying around; 'Billy Rampatter' and 'Spare Pie' – "Work a half shift and dinnet tell yer mate", said the gaffer.
"Oh that's handy I've got a spare pie in my haversack."

And, there was 'The Wizard'

who was always saying: "Lets have a spell."

The shipyards weren't places for sensitive people. Some couldn't take the humour and left. It was said that the banter was the way hard, cynical men showed their approval of a workmate. It was a strange show of affection indeed!

However, some men who were the main culprits of the p___ taking entertainment couldn't take it themselves. And when they were on the receiving end threats were sometimes heard by school bullies who had overflowed from the playground and into the shipyards!

Friendly rivalry (and sometimes unfriendly rivalry) existed between outfitting trades and boilermakers at Pickies. There were some good boilermaker jokes like the boilermaker who went to the TSB on The Green to draw out £8. He had three attempts to spell 'eight' on the cheque but failed each time. He finally tore up the cheque, wrote another one out for £10 and put £2 back into his account.

Class discrimination existed on the shop floor at Pickies. On one occasion there was a rush job in the shed and a squad of platers and platers helpers were asked to work a half shift overtime at short notice. The gaffer sent an apprentice to the fish shop for their tea. The order was for fish lots for the platers and pattie lots for the helpers.

The cleaning department had two well known characters. On one occasion the foreman sent 'Bonnie Ronnie' to sweep the bridge (meaning the bridge on the ship at the quayside). He was later spotted sweeping the path on the Alexandra Bridge.

Tommy Harvey (Tashy) was employed at sweeping the fabrication shed and he was a target for the tormentors. On one occasion he complained to a manager: "I'm sick of this brush. The head has fell off twice and now the shaft's come out!"

One day his wheel barrow's tyre punctured. Tommy decided to carry it on his back to the garage to get repaired. On his journey through the yard, scrap metal, lugs and other objects were thrown into the barrow. By the time he reached the garage his legs were buckling under the weight.

One morning when he came to work he couldn't find his precious wheel barrow. The night shift had put it on top of the shed roof.

Tommy was always keen to show off his strength. He was challenged to try to lift his own weight by standing in two buckets. His face reddened by the extra exertion provoked by taunts from the crowd that had assembled to witness the feat of strength: "You cannot even lift your own weight, Tommy."

Prior to returning to work after a spell of sickness it was the practice to visit the yard to inform the foreman. One day in the early 1980s Tommy walked into the shed wearing a pair of large, brilliant white Cuban heel shoes or boots which someone must have given to him. The whole shed came to a standstill as men shouted and wolf whistled at him.

Tommy had a reputation as a good worker and despite the 'mickey taking' many men looked after him. Some provided him with clothes and shoes while others gave him left over bait and tins of food.

Tommy idolised Elvis and often did impersonations of his hero. Southwick Social Club held a talent contest every Monday night in about the late 1970s / early 1980s, and Tommy entered as Elvis. The event was well publicised at Pickies and in Southwick pubs were Tommy was well known. The concert room was packed and

Tommy did not disappoint his followers. His Elvis mannerisms and gyrations onstage complemented one or two lines of Elvis' greatest hits which Tommy composed into one song. "He brought the house down," recalls Sammy Hall. Tommy won the talent contest easily.

One of the memorable occasions at the Southwick shipyard was the visit by the Queen as part of 'Her Majesty's Silver Jubilee Tour' in 1977. Preparations had gone on for months when the yard was cleaned up and painted. It was estimated that over 3,500 people, including many school children waving Union Jack flags, waited for the Queen to arrive. There was great disappointment, however, when the royal motorcade passed through the yard without stopping. It was said at the time that there was a fleeting glimpse and a royal wave to Tommy Harvey. The photograph (minus the Queen's words of course) appeared in the September 1977 issue of A&P News. Someone

recorded what the Queen had said to Phillip and copies of the incident appeared on noticeboards in the yard.

Foremen and managers were fair game for banter among the men. There was 'Head and Shoulders' who tried to avoid entering confined spaces. He would pop his head down a tank to enquire about the progress of a job. There was 'Mick the Mute' who didn't speak to anybody; 'Chocolate Soldier'; and it was tough luck not to be one of 'Lal's Pals'. 'Pampers' was a manager in the shed. He was a very young whizz kid and still in nappies. But perhaps the most infamous was 'YoYo' the manager who was always rushing up and down various parts of the ship. On one occasion 'YoYo' had been chalked in large letters on the forend where the ship's name was normally placed. It was hilarious as crowds assembled for the launch. YoYo was overheard asking another manager who YoYo was. "It's you man. You daft _____." Was the reply.

Regulars of the Smiths Arms in the 1970s. Left to right: Jackie Carlisle, Tommy Harvey, Walter Henry.

# Southwick Shipyard Characters

## Illustrated
## by
## Pal Palmer

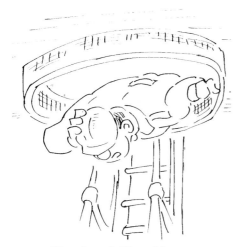

**Head and Shoulders**
"Neet shift done much lads?"

**YoYo**
He was always up and down

I'll work the half shift, Gaffer. I just happen to have a spare pie in my haversack.

**Spare Pie**
Liked his overtime and was always prepared for the unexpected shift.

**Kittens**
So named because of his habit of pawing the remains of his meal away like a kitten.

**Chicken George**
A workman left his meal to go for a drink. When he returned a man sitting nearby had assumed he wasn't coming back and was eating his chicken leg. The series 'Roots' was on TV at the time.

**Hollywood Welder**
A poser who was often seen with a packet of welding rods on his shoulder, but was rarely caught welding.

**The Drill**
A complete and utter bore.

**Bonnie Ronnie**
"Isn't that the new starter you told to sweep the ship's bridge Gaffer?"

**Baldy Mouth**

**Tommy Tomato**
Amateur gardener, professional crawler.

**The Body (a layabout)**
"He was there at breaktime cos I chalked him in for a laugh."

**The Flattener**
He looked after the shower block and was a horse race enthusiast. He received the results on his radio and seemed to take a delight to let you know your bet was flat.

**"The gran who launched a thousand chips"** was a newspaper headline in December 1979, when local and national media attention was focused on 52-year-old canteen assistant Iris Lindsay. Iris' name had been drawn out of a hat full of A&P's female employees names to launch the SD14 *Luc-Nam*. The Vietnamese owners decided not to send anyone to launch the ship – hence the lucky draw. It was the tradition of the yard that a female launched the ships.

"It was very exciting," recalled 69-year-old Iris at her home at Doxford Park. "They sent a chauffeur driven car for me. The chauffeur was dressed in uniform. When the car arrived at the yard workmen waved to me. I saw Margaret and Lilian whom I worked with on nightshift in the canteen. They waved to me and I waved back. I felt like royalty. I was a Queen for a day."

The canteen opened on nightshift in the late 1970s when Bartram's closed and the workforce was transferred to Southwick. Iris volunteered for nightshift: "I think it must have been a bit of a novelty when a group of women started on nightshift at Pickies," said Iris. "I had been a housewife with six kids and I was a bit naive. We took some stick with the nightshift's own brand of humour. One night Margaret received a phone call that a coach full of passengers had broken down, and could we help by serving them all a meal. Questions were asked about prices and the menu. The caller said he would phone back with the exact numbers. We wanted to help them and we frantically assessed the amount of food we had in stock. Margaret received another call and she found out that the 'coach rep' was a nightshift welder. Margaret did her nut with him.

"There was a lot of mickey taking on nightshift but they were good lads and they were kind to us at Christmas. We had a good laugh and the girls and I enjoyed our work at Pickies."

*The Luc-Nam and the crowd wait for Iris.*

*Overlooked by Derek Kimber, Chairman of the Board of Directors of A&P, Iris pressed the button to launch the ship.*

*Above: The press and television crews wanted to know more about the grandmother who launched the ship. Right: Happy times on nightshift at Pickies. Canteen workers left to right: Iris Lindsay, Margaret Charlton and Lilian Anderson with foreman welder Billy Cole.*

*The SD14 slips into the river.*

# Memories of Pickersgill's
## by Leslie Tate

I started work at Pickersgill's in April 1939 with the stocktakers. I was fourteen-years-old and I operated a crane for stacking plates. All of the steel was brought into the yard by horse and cart from Southwick Goods Yard by the contractor J. Prior. Horses and carts were also used in the yard in those days. They were the internal transport.

The toilet facilities were very primitive in 1939. It seems hard to believe what we had to do when compared with today's standards. There was a jetty protruding from the shoreline and overhanging the river. The structure stood on shores and a walkway led to a large plank. We parked our bottoms over the end of the plank and did our business into the river at high tide, or onto the sleck at low tide. There was no privacy or separate compartments as men sat next to each other on the plank. We had to take our own newspaper and that was done in front of the others as well. It was difficult to get a place on the plank on Monday mornings when men had the skitters after a weekend of boozing. You could be seated next to a rough riveter who was trying to nudge his way in: "Howay young'un. Gerralang a bit!"

The toilets were a shocking experience for me as a young lad and it took some getting used to. I had heard that on some occasions apprentices got onto the shoreline at low tide beneath 'the plank' and pelted the bare backsides with sleck.

*September 3rd, 1939* – War was declared. Nothing seemed to change in the shipyard other than air raid shelters being built.

*October 14th* – A Saturday at midday I heard that the Royal Oak had been sunk at Scapa Flow with a large loss of life. No news of brother William, aged 21. Then early on Sunday morning whilst delivering newspapers I saw the latest list of survivors in the Stop Press. I was overjoyed when I saw my brothers name – William Tate. He was in hospital in Invergordon and father and mother went to see him after being told that he was seriously ill. They found him absolutely black with total burns and covered with fuel oil. William said, "I got out for you mother." When the first torpedo hit the ship there was a big bang but no apparent damage. Being off duty he ran up onto the deck with other crew members but they were ordered below by the Duty Officer as there was nothing to be seen. William had settled down again when the next torpedoes hit and turned it over. William managed to get out of a porthole underwater, and swam to the surface where fuel oil was on fire.

He was rescued but over 800 men died that night. Father was worried about his job and the cost of staying at Invergordon. He returned home. Immediately a yard meeting was called in the platers' shed, when it was agreed that each man would donate 2/6d (12½p) to pay for my fathers return to Invergordon. The money was paid in advance by Pickersgill's so my father could leave immediately for Scotland. My brother died on Friday 27th October 1939. His funeral was said at the time to have been the biggest ever seen in Southwick. William was buried with full military honours (see also page 62).

*June 1940* – I was working in the Power House as a fifteen-year-old apprentice electrician. Two Army Officers came to the Power House because of possible German invasion after the conquest of France. The two large air compressors which supplied the compressed air for the shipyard power tools had to be immobilised when not in use. This was done by taking the brush gear off the electric motors and placing it into a special sealed box. In the event of an invasion the compressors were to be put out of action by the Army taking charge of the brush gear. I was given a special Army pass and went to Jerome's in High Street to have my photograph taken to include in the pass. I was chosen because the Army Officials said that the Germans would take less notice of me because of my age.

*November 1940* – Fire watches were formed at Pickersgill's. They were on a rota and on duty one night per week incase air raid fires started in the yard. They later moved from the old canteen to the old Times Inn building outside of the yard.

*1942* – I joined Pickersgill's Home Guard unit. Kit Cunningham was Lieutenant. Tommy Cunningham and Billy Spoors were Sergeants. Duties included rifle practice at Whitburn; Mills bomb practice with fuses at Fulwell quarry and all night guards at Dykelands Road Drill Hall. The guard ended with a bus home at 6 am to start work for a full day at 7.30 am. A fine body of men defending the country against invasion.

*1942* – William Pickersgill came into the Power House one day and said: "Come on we are going for a run out." We travelled in his car to Newcastle to pick up the Billmeir Cup which had been engraved there. In wartime a car could not be left unattended unless it was immobilised. This meant taking off the distributor cover, removing the arm and taking it with you. By taking me with him William Pickersgill did not have to do that.

William Pickersgill who was the head of the firm,

was known by the workmen as 'Mr William'. He was well thought of by the men. He was a gentleman and well mannered. He was regularly in close contact with the men on the shop floor, and on occasions during the 1930s, while on board a vessel under construction, he would take off his coat and knock down a few rivets. Mr William was approachable and he had time for people. He cared about his workmen and would ask how our family's were getting on. He took a pride in knowing all his employees by their first names. All of this helped to create a good atmosphere in the yard.

*Late 1943* – I went to reopen the West Yard, which was Priestman's old yard that had been closed for several years. Fifteen-year-old Arthur Dodd worked with me and we made up all of the welding gear, the ships temporary lighting equipment and carried out all of the maintenance and repairs. Eighteen-year-old Joan Cowley looked after the Power House and the compressor in the reopened yard. Joan like many other women had started work as a labourer at Pickersgill's owing to the shortage of men who were with the Armed Forces.

Mr William, while on a walk around the yard had a chat with me and said: "You know the Americans with their prefabricated ships. You cannot build good ships like that."

*1944* – I won the Billmeir Cup as the Best Apprentice of the Year. I think it was because I had been working in the West Yard for some time as a full electrician.

*March 26th, 1947* – I was married to Joan Cowley and Arthur Dodd was the Best Man.

Above – Les Tate being presented with the Billmeir Cup in 1944 by Rear Admiral Maxwell in the presence of his fellow apprentices. William Pickersgill is in the centre wearing the bowler.

Left – Letter from William Pickersgill informing Les Tate of his achievement.

# Demolition!

The Southwick Shipyard is silent. Berths are empty and Wearsiders hope for a last minute reprieve.

Demolition of the yard begins in February 1991. The 'old' prefabrication shed is flattened.

Work starts to dismantle the covered in berths ('the new complex').

Cranes topple and the railway into the yard (foreground) has been lifted.

The covered in berths are stripped.

The 'old shed' and berth cranes have been burnt up and lie neatly in piles. The 'new' prefabrication shed (right) and the mangle shed (foreground) are dismantled.

The new complex is flattened.

The sheds have almost disappeared.

The demolition crew open out a fine view of the river.

1

2

5

7

3

4

6

9

10

8

11

12

13

14

17

15

16

20

18

21

22

23

24

**Captions for pages 98 & 99**

1. Victorian post box positioned in the wall opposite Fitzroy Terrace at West Southwick.
2. The Robert Thompson Memorial on The Green on January 22nd 1984.
3. Inscription on the north side of the Thompson Memorial.
4. The Thompson family crest – An armoured arm holding a reversed broken lance, and the motto – "Dum Spiro Spero" ("While I have breath I hope").
5. A large unevenly shaped brick was recovered from a demolition site in Villiers Street, Sunderland in 1995. William Dodd Pratt owned a brickworks at Southwick. He was also the first chairman of Southwick Local Board when the local government was established in 1863.
6. Sewer grating or cover bearing the title 'Southwick on Wear U.D. Council'. Sewer covers similar to this one at Scott's Bank can be seen at the older parts of Southwick.
7. This boundary stone was fitted above the doorway of this house (109 Southwick Road) when the row of colliery houses was built in the 1890s. The stone bears the Sunderland Corporation Crest and the letters MB (Municipal Boundary). The stone defined the boundary between Sunderland and Southwick Urban District.
8. The steps at the top of Newbold Avenue in Monkwearmouth led to Boundary Street in Southwick (pictured in 1984). The Boundary Street name plate can be seen on the gable end house but the plate has been removed recently.
9. This building at the riverside survived the demolition of Southwick Bottleworks. Picture taken in 1996.
10. On the site of Robert Thompson's shipyard the initials RT are roughly engraved into a stone block, and above the date 1875.
11. Limekilns existed at this site in the late 1700s. Possibly some of the original kilns survive in this row today.
12. The date 1821 can be seen on an arch which originally provided an entrance for coal to fuel the limekilns. (See Southwick on Wear Vol. 1 P. 12).
13. Cornhill Dock in 1981 shortly before it was levelled during a reclamation scheme.
14. The Thistle C.I.U. Workmen's Club in 1984 before it became the Dagmar pub.
15. Centre, is the air raid siren at Cato Street NEEB Sub Station. Occasional tests were carried out in the 1950s and '60s, and the deafening wailing noise made a new generation aware of the possibility of a new war breaking out. The houses on the right were rebuilt after they were demolished by a bomb in 1941 (see page 49).
16. Plate from the Labour Exchange on The Green. The premises are now a Chinese Takeaway.
17. A stone in the doorway commemorates the opening of the Council Offices by Robert Thompson's wife.
18. 'The Old Town Hall' was opened by the Mayor Councillor Bryan Charlton on March 28th 1994 after a major restoration of the building. The stone mason is pictured putting the finishing touches to the inscription at the doorway on the day before the opening ceremony.
19. The Old Town Hall on March 28th 1994.
20. The Burton House pub in Wear Street lost its licence in 1930. A faded advert survived on the building until recent years when it was faced with concrete. The advert reads: 'William McEwans Mild'.
21. The burial place of William Pickersgill the shipbuilder in Holy Trinity Churchyard. He was killed in 1880 when on board a vessel under construction. A shore unexpectedly fell and crushed his head.
22. A 'Stone bottle' pulled out of the sleck at Southwick riverside by Michael Henry.
23. Beaumont Street shops on December 30th 1983. Since then the fish shop on the south side and the butchers on the north side have been demolished. The post box and telephone kiosk have been removed.
24. Special mugs were made for the Southwick-on-Wear celebrations to commemorate the Coronation of George V in 1911.

## Timber Beach
### by Paul Mortimer
### Durham Wildlife Trust

Timber Beach is the name of the Durham Wildlife Trust's nature reserve on the river bank at Southwick. Its name is derived from shipbuilding days, when rafts of timber were towed up the river and lashed to the tidal mudflats next to the shipyards. Here the timber was seasoned in the brackish tidal water before being used in the yards. At low tide the timbers would rest upon the mud to become literally a timber beach.

The brackish nature of the water, a mixture of salty incoming sea water and fresh water draining from inland, has given rise to some very rare habitat, which has been of interest to naturalists since the beginning of this century. Where there is a level river bank which is only occasionally covered by the tide, certain specialist plants are able to thrive and create a habitat called *saltmarsh*. These plants are specially adapted to this salty environment by having thick waxy leaves to survive the dehydrating effect of the salt.

Before the industrialisation of the

*Timber Beach at Southwick in 1996.*

*Tide and weather have exposed sandstone and created a beach at Southwick.*

north east, much of the Wear estuary would have been bounded by saltmarsh, providing vital feeding grounds for huge numbers of birds. The pressure for land for shipbuilding resulted in most of this being reclaimed from the river and subsequently built upon. The saltmarsh at Timber Beach is just a tiny fragment of what was once here, and this makes its protection even more vital.

A walk around Timber Beach will reveal many more natural treasures. Just down river from the saltmarsh the crumbling river cliffs are the first section of natural river bank to be met as one travels inland. The top of the cliffs is made of boulder clay left by glaciers in the last ice age. This clay is very weak and occasionally collapses into the river. At the foot of the cliff is much older sandstone. Geologists call this Permian Yellow Sand, and are able to tell that it is about 250 million years old. If you look at it closely under a magnifying glass, you will see that the individual grains of sand are quite rounded and have a frosted surface texture. This tells us that this sandstone was originally desert sand dunes, the frosting being a result of the sand grains rubbing against each other in the wind. The idea of

Southwick being a desert seems extraordinary, but about 240 million years ago, this desert was flooded by water to form the Zechstein Sea. Southwick was located near the western edge of this sea which stretched across into Northern Europe. In the shallow, warm tropical waters of this sea coral reefs began to grow on top of the sandstone. You can see part of this reef today at the top half of Claxheugh Rock on the south side of the river, and at Bunny Hill, overlooking Hylton Castle.

On top of the cliffs above Timber Beach are some wonderful meadows, full of wild flowers. These are what is left of the farmland which once dominated this area. As they have never been subject to intensive modern farming methods, an unusually rich mixture of plants has survived. Their names reflect their old countyside origins: cowslip, fleabane, adders-tongue, meadowsweet. These meadows provide a home to a huge range of insects and small mammals which in turn feed a large population of breeding birds. Some of these birds fly from as far away as North Africa to nest in the bushes of Southwick.

In 1991 the Durham Wildlife Trust joined forces with the Tyne and Wear

Development Corporation to protect this special part of Sunderland. A project officer was appointed to both look after the wildlife and to encourage local people to come and enjoy it. New footpaths were built to open up the riverside to everyone, and a range of improvements carried out to make the riverside a cleaner, more pleasant place.

The future survival of special places such as this lies in the hands of our young people. To this end, Tyne and Wear Development Corporation funded the production of a teacher's pack of information and activities based on the riverside. Thousands of schoolchildren now visit the riverside as part of their curriculum studies to learn about its history and natural treasures.

### The Meerstones

In the 1820s/30s the River Wear Commissioners placed meerstones at intervals from the river's mouth up to Hylton at the high tide level. The line of stones indicated the RWC's jurisdiction. That is, everything on the river's side of the stones was their responsibility. Prior to that period industrialists and others had been building structures which hindered river traffic. The meerstones created an instant check that people were obeying the regulations. However, applications to build beyond the meerstones could be approved by the RWC at a charge on occasion.

Very few meerstones exist today but there are several at Timber Beach like the one pictured above. (Information about the meerstones has been obtained from historian Stuart Miller)

*Nature Park at the riverside within the boundaries of old Southwick.*

Regulars playing dominos in the Conservative Club in 1984. (Photograph by Billy Donkin)

Left: The Conservative Club in 1984.

Excavations took place in 1990 and 1992 by the archaeology section of Tyne and Wear Museums and funded by Sunderland Borough Council. Ditches were dug in a field immediately north of Earlston Street on the Carley Hill Estate within the old boundaries of Southwick Township. The field is on high ground and, unlike the surrounding area, it has not been quarried over recent centuries. The excavations revealed one of the earliest settlement sites in Northern Britain. Steve Speak , Keeper of Field Archaeology wrote of the find: " … However, one of the most fundamental concern was the accidental discovery of the site whilst exploring the pattern of post Medieval ridge and furrow ploughing." The remains of a turf bank was found and at the bottom of a 0.60m ditch there was a layer of cobbles, from where charcoal was extracted and gave a radio-carbon date of 80 BC. What was even more interesting, however, pottery sealed below the cobbles was found to date from the Bronze Age period of about 1,000 BC.

Following the Meadow Well Estate riots on North Tyneside, when poverty and deprivation were said to have been the root of the problems, other riots occurred in the north of England. On Friday 13th September 1991 two squads of riot police dispersed a gang of about twenty youths who had barricaded Beaumont Street with burning rubbish and had stoned police vehicles.

A stone axe unearthed at Austin and Pickersgill's Southwick Shipyard during a modernisation programme in 1976 is now in Sunderland Museum. The axe is Neolithic (4,000 - 2,400 BC). A period which is also known as The New Stone Age.

H.R.H. Diana The Princess of Wales arrives at Southwick to open St Columba's Parish Centre on June 27th, 1990. After the opening ceremony and the unveiling of a commemorative plaque, the Rev Martin Saunders presents The Princess of Wales with bound volumes of the Southwick-on-Wear books.

# Subscribers

1. May Foster
2. Tom Marshall
3. Lorna Storey
4. Mickey Butler
5. Betty & Wilf Meechin
6. Olga & Tom Meechin
7. Michael Gibson
8. Mr H. Holcroft
9. Mr A. Stamp
10. Anne Ray
11. Kathleen Fenwick
12. Catherine Young
13. Ethel Wilson
14. Ella Ridley
15. Mr E.W. Atkinson
16. Mr A. Atkinson
17. P. Philpot
18. Ron Bell
19. Freda McCowliff
20. Miss V. Bambrough
21. Mr J. Bambrough
22. Mrs B. Wardle
23. David Evans
24. John L. Walton
25. Mr K. Lay
26. Mr J. Lay
27. Jack Robson
28. H. Bennett
29. Mr N. Catcherside
30. J.W. Noble
31. Lt-Col. B.S. Brazier
32. Kathleen Cowell
33. Roy Horabin
34. Teresa Pallas
35. Norma Crozier
36. Hilda Cullen
37. David Warne
38. Elsie Forbister
39. Leslie & Joan Tate
40. Pamela Tate
41. Marilyn Joan Campbell
42. Andrew Campbell
43. Victoria Joanne Campbell
44. Jonathon Leslie Campbell
45. Arthur E. Dodd
46. Samuel Barkes Forbister
47. William Forbister
48. Robert Hope Forbister
49. James & Martha Forbister
50. Ron & Irene Forbister
51. Ella & Ron Middleton
52. Joseph & Ethel Sheriff
53. Audrey Carruthers
54. Evelyn McDonald
55. Tony & Jenny Cooke
56. Gordon & Irene Cook
57. Mr R.J. Churchill
58. Brian Duffell
59. Mr I. Applegarth
60. Robert Schonewald
61. Mrs E.M. Cook
62. Mrs K. Biglow
63. Mrs K. Williams
64. Mr & Mrs A. Greenhow
65. Roger Norris
66. Mrs Audrey Dent
67. Mrs E.A. King
68. G. Pyburn
69. Mrs Marie Foster
70. James Foster
71. Mr D.W. Jeffrey
72. Ronnie Green
73. Norman Hedinburgh
74. Mr B. Scott
75. Mrs Vera Wood
76. Anne W. Thompson
77. M.D. Gardiner
78. L. Marsh
79. Mrs M. Fisher
80. C.R. Riddell
81. Arthur Turnbull
82. Mr H.D. Bell
83. Mary McQuillan
84. Mr R.G. Pace
85. D. Heptinstall
86. L. Cooper
87. Mr A. Ibbitson
88. Mrs J. Birkett
89. Mr J. Sheriff
90. Mr & Mrs L. Hodgson
91. A.J. Cowell
92. Mrs M. Vierow
93. Stanley Heavisides
94. J.R. Salkeld
95. Mr W.C. Taylor
96. Mrs Betty Wilson
97. Mrs E. Smith
98. Malcolm Gray
99. Mr & Mrs Alf Davison
100. Mrs Lilian Fletcher
101. James Henry Stridiron
102. Norman Hildrew
103. Mr & Mrs J.E. Clark
104. Charles H. Carter
105. Mrs E.L. Richardson
106. Mrs M. Hodgson
107. Sunderland Museum & Art Gallery
108. Neil Sinclair, Sunderland Museum
109. Mrs B. Marshall
110. Mrs T. Hopps
111. Leslie Sheriff
112. Wilf Sheriff
113. Maurice Sheriff
114. Capt. Sam Irving
115. Mrs E.A. Irving
116. Meg & John Robertson
117. Mrs Maureen C. Hurst
118. Mrs Joan Morris
119. Mrs Sheila Wilson
120. R.M. Laybourn
121. Mr & Mrs J.W. Wilkinson
122. William Cleghorn Terry
123. Mr J. Graham
124. Mr & Mrs H. Richardson
125. Mrs L. Johnson
126. Emma S. Jackson
127. Ron Giles
128. Mr T. Greenhow
129. Pat O'Brien
130. Margaret Thynne
131. R. Jeffrey
132. J. Maidment
133. W. Maidment
134. Eric Young
135. Wesley Young
136. J.R. Elwen
137. Mrs Linda Liddell
138. Bob Robinson
139. Gorden Aslett
140. Master Charles Butler
141. Master K.C. Brown
142. Mr W.F. MacPherson
143. Mr T. Ditch
144. Stan Fowler
145. Fred Wardropper
146. Rene Stewart
147. James E. Potts
148. Mrs E. Hetherington
149. Mrs J. Stephenson
150. Joyce Starbuck
151. Mr J. Taylor
152. Jean Stacey
153. Molly Todd
154. Harry Bruce
155. Father John Troop
156. Peter Hudson
157. Miss M. Gladwin
158. Beryl Howard
159. Janette Hylton
160. Miss M. Lennon
161. Mrs Hilary Forrester
162. Mrs Sally Collins
163. Mary Cairns
164. Tony Thompson (senior)
165. Jack Washington
166. Frederick Parkes
167. Mrs M. Storey
168. Jim McGoff
169. Mr G.B. Luke
170. Dr K.D. Luke
171. Roxanne Mutch
172. Robert Langley
173. Keith Oxman
174. Jimmy Langley
175. Mrs Lynda Davison
176. Sharon Sallabank
177. Doreen Sallabank

178. Sheila Little
179. Miss Julie Rain
180. Geo. W. Graham
181. Peter Aslett
182. Rev R. Dixon, the Rectory Southwick
183. Mrs Molly Vincett
184. Mr & Mrs Raymond Reed
185. Mrs Edith Messerich
186. Mr Chris Williams &
    Mrs Sheila Forster
187. Una Norman

188. Jack Lowes
189. Harry J. Henry
190. Cara Hawes
191. Mrs Nora Wilson
192. Chris Hall
193. June Ainsley
194. Jim & Anne Douglas
195. George Holmes
196. George & Tot Gibson
197. George Simpson
198. Mrs Esther Gibson

199. Doris Jones (nee Duffell)
200. Robert Lythgoe Hopps
201. Rhoda Leonard
202. Mrs Audrey Carrick
203. Mrs Margaret Porter
204. Peter M. Gibson
205. Victoria L. Gibson
206. Mark J. Gibson
207. Joan Talabani-Gibson
208. Mrs Irene Gibson

---

## CAN YOU HELP?

Although this is the last book in the Southwick-on-Wear series I intend to continue researching and writing local history. I will be interested to hear from you if you have information or interesting family snaps or photographs of street scenes, buildings, social events, war etc. of the following areas: Monkwearmouth, Southwick, Fulwell, Roker and Seaburn. Photographs can be copied at your home.

If you can help please contact me:

Peter Gibson
100 Newcastle Road
Sunderland
SR5 1JJ
Telephone: (0191) 548 3228

Two Southwick children on Roker beach in 1981. Have you interesting photographs taken at Roker and Seaburn?

*Back cover*

*Top left:* Naval Commando John T. Bland's medals from World War II. Far left is his Distinguished Service Medal. (see page 61).
*Top right:* Southwick Mill in 1878. Painted by Jim Keers in 1991 from a faded photograph. The mill was demolished in 1879 to make way for Gordon Terrace.
*Middle left:* HRH Diana, The Princess of Wales is greeted on her arrival at Southwick on June 27th 1990 to open St Columba's Parish Centre. See front cover and page 102.
*Middle right:* Southwick House at the east end of The Green in about 1905. The Scott family who owned the pottery lived there. The last occupier was Dr Dickey and his family (see page 31). Southwick House was demolished in 1962.
*Bottom left:* Austin Pickersgill's Shipyard flag was saved during the demolition of the yard in 1991. The flag is displayed at Marley Pots in March 1996.
*Bottom right:* Remembrance Sunday 1995 at Southwick Cenotaph in the 50th anniversary year of the ending of World War II. After a wreath had been laid on behalf of the members of Southwick Social Club two minutes silence was observed. Beside the wreath was a bunch of flowers with a simple message attached – "To my two pals, killed in Germany 6-4-1945. 4th Batt. Welsh Reg-BLA."